Some Nests of Birds, Insects and Animals

Mary Titcomb

ISBN 9781477653920

©2012
Folly Cove 01930
Gloucester MA

www.follycove.biz

Singing Honey Eater   Painted Honey Eater
                    Yellow Throated Sericornis
White Honey Eater   Rock Warbler

No style of architecture, either ancient or modern, presents specimens of more curious beauty and delicacy than the ingenuous structures which many of the feathered tribes build for their habitations. They too, as well as man, have their various orders and styles; among which the hanging nests are especially unique and interesting. All the pensile birds are remarkable for the eccentricity of shape and design which marks their nests; although they agree in one point—namely, that they dangle at the end of twigs, and dance about merrily at every breeze. Some of them are very long, others are very short; some have their entrance at the side, others from below, and others again from near the top. Some are hung, hammock-like, from one twig to another; other are suspended to the extremity of the twig itself; while others, that build in the palms, which have no true branches, and no twigs at all, fasten their nests to the extremities of the leaves. Some are made of various fibers, and others of the coarsest grass-straws: some are so loose in their texture, that the eggs can be plainly seen through them; while others are so strong and thick that they almost look as if they were made by a professional thatcher.

The Tailer Bird

The individual who first invented sewing, doubtless thought he had discovered, or rather created, an entirely new art; although, indeed, the respectable fraternity of tailors were wont to attribute to their mystery an antiquity surpassing that of any other handicraft, and, on the strength of a certain passage in Genesis, claimed Adam as the first tailor. Had they been moderately skilled in ornithology, they might have claimed a still older origin, on the grounds that, long before man came on the earth, the needle and the thread were used for sewing two objects together.

Swallow Dicaeum

The wonderful little bird, whose portrait is accurately given in the accompanying illustration, is popularly known by the appropriate title of Tailor Bird, and is a native of India. The manner in which it constructs its pensile nest is very singular. Choosing a convenient leaf, generally one which hangs from the end of a slender twig, it pierces a row of holes along each edge, using its beak in the same manner that a shoemaker uses his awl, the two instruments being very similar to each other in shape, though not in material. These holes are not at all regulars and in some cases there are so many of them, that the bird seems to have found some special gratification in making them, just as a boy who has a new knife makes havoc on every piece of wood which he can obtain.

Lanceolate Honey Eater

When the holes are completed, the bird next procures its thread, which is a long fiber of some plant; generally much longer than is needed for the task which it performs. Having found its thread, the feathered tailor begins to pass it through the holes, drawing the sides of the leaf toward each other, so as to form a kind of hollow cone, the point downward. Generally a single leaf is used for this purpose, but whenever the bird can not find one that is sufficiently large, it sews two together, or even fetches another leaf and fastens it with the fiber. Within the hollow thus formed the bird next deposits a quantity of soft white down, like short cotton wool, and thus constructs a warm, light, and elegant nest, which is scarcely visible among the leafage of the tree, and which is safe from almost every foe except man.

There is another pretty bird, the Fan-Tailed Warbler, which sews leaves together to form a nest, although that nest can not be ranked among the pensiles. This bird builds among reeds, sewing together a number of their flat blades, in order to make a hollow wherein its nest may be hidden. Instead, however, of passing its thread continuously through the holes, it has a great number of threads, and makes a knot at the end of each, in order to prevent it from being pulled through the hole.

Some very remarkable examples of pensile birds' nests are found in Australia. In the more dense and humid parts of the Australian forests there is a rapid and abundant growth of moss upon the trunks of decayed trees, and even it often accumulates in large masses at the extremities of the drooping branches. These masses often become of sufficient size to admit of the Yellow-throated Sericornis constructing a nest in the center of them, which it does with so much art that it is impossible to distinguish it from any of the other pendulous masses in the vicinity. These bunches are frequently a yard in length; and although the nest is constantly disturbed by the wind, and liable to be shaken when the tree is disturbed, so secure does the inmate consider itself from danger or intrusion of any kind, that the female is frequently captured while sitting on her eggs—a feat that may always be accomplished by carefully placing the hand over the entrance—that is, if it can be detected, to effect which no slight degree of close prying and examination is necessary. The nest is formed of the inner bark of trees, intermingled with green moss, which soon vegetates; sometimes dried grasses and fibrous roots form part of the materials of which it is composed, and it is warmly lined with feathers.

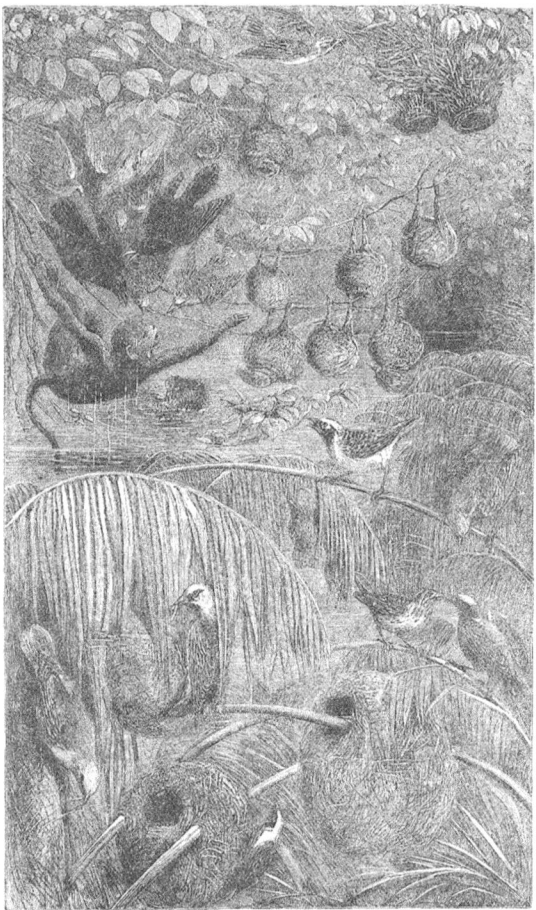

African Weaver

The Rock Warbler or Cataract Bird, so called because it is always found where water-courses rush through rocky ground, claims special admiration in consequence of the extraordinary nest which it builds. In general shape it somewhat resembles a claret jug, without a handle, having a long slender neck, and a globular and suddenly rounded bulb. It is suspended from the rocks in sheltered places, wherever an overhanging ledge affords protection. The entrance is near the center of the bulb, and though the nest is very rough on the exterior, it is smooth and comfortable enough within.

A most beautiful pensile nest is made by the Singing Honey-Eater in a common Australian tree, popularly called the Myall. The twigs of this tree are long and very slender, and the leaves are so narrow and delicate that at a little distance they look more like grass-blades than the leaf of a tree. The long and slender twigs serve the double purpose of affording a firm attachment for the nest and suspending it where no ordinary foe can reach it, while the delicate leaves give their aid in fastening the nest to the twigs, and at the same time serve to conceal the structure from prying eyes. The nest is made of grasses, which although green when first woven, become white and dry in a short time. The grass is mingled with hair, which, matted together, make it impervious to wind and rain.

The Painted Honey-Eater, a native of New South Wales, is a handsome bird of rich brown color above, with the exception of a yellow patch on the base of the tail, and white, slightly spotted below. A characteristic mark of the species is a little patch of pure white just by the ears. This species does not confine itself merely to a diet of sweet juices, but feeds much on small insects. The birds are generally seen in pairs, and are very playful, chasing each other merrily, and spreading their tails so as to show the white color. They sit on a branch, keeping a careful watch, and whenever an insect passes near, they dart into the air, catch it, and return to their post. The nest of the Painted Honey-Eater is a beautiful example of the pensiles. So also is that of the White-throated Honey-eater, whose curious nest, about as large as a breakfast-cup, and very much of the same shape, is made of delicate paper like bark and various vegetable fibers, with which it is ingeniously hung to the branches. The broad, thin bark causes it to be very smooth on the exterior. For the lining, the bird is not indebted to any animal or bird, but uses grass-blades, which are neatly laid, and form a soft resting place for the eggs. The nest, which is placed low, is always hung near the extremity of a branch, in such a position as to be under the protection of a spray of leaves, which act as a roof whereby the rain is thrown off.

Sociable Weaver Bird

These five singular Australian nests, which have been described, have been placed together in our opening illustration, and, may be compared with each other at a glance.

Nests of Birds, Insects and Animals

The Swallow Dicaeum is a bird scarcely as large as our common wren, and glowing with brilliant colors, the whole of the upper part being deep, glossy blue-black; the throat, breast, and under tail-coverts of a fiery scarlet; and the abdomen pure white. It has a very sweet though low and inward note, so faint as scarcely to be audible from the tops of the trees, but continued for a long time together.

Artificial aids to vision are required in order to watch the habits of the Dicaeum, for it loves the tops of the tallest trees, where its minute body can scarcely be seen without the assistance of glasses. Its nest is as pretty as the architect, and its ordinary shape can be seen in the illustration, though the plain black and white of a wood engraving can give but little idea of its full beauty. In color it is nearly pure white, being made of the cotton like down which protects the seeds of many plants; and this material. is so artfully woven that the nest almost looks as if made from a piece of very white cloth. It is always purse-like in form, and is suspended by the upper portion to the twigs at the very summit of the tree.

We next mention a bird which may be accepted as the first hammock-maker, its nest being made of a hammock-like shape, and slung just as a seaman slings his oscillating couch. Scarcely any more comfortable bed could be invented, provided that it be properly suspended; and the bird certainly deserves our gratitude, if it be only for the fact that it might have given the first hint on the subject. It is called the Lanceolate Honey-Eater, on account of the shape of its feathers. It does not seem to be a very lively bird, and is so still and quiet that it would hardly be seen were not its presence betrayed by an occasional powerful and shrilly sounding whistle. The wonderful nest of this bird was discovered by a naturalist, in the Liverpool Plains, overhanging a stream. The material of which it is made are grass and wool, intermingled with the pure white cotton of certain flowers. As the reader may see, by reference to the illustration, it is hung from a very slender twig, and only suspended at opposite extremities of the rim the tree selected being the myall, or weeping acacia. The nest is rather small in proportion to the bird, and is very deep, so that when the mother is sitting on her eggs, or brooding over her young, she is obliged to pack herself away very carefully, her tail projecting at one side of the nest and her head at the other.

Little Hermit

Although the majority of nest-making birds may be called Weavers, there is one family to which the name, is peculiarly appropriate, and they are all inhabitants of the hot portions of the old world, chiefly Asia and Africa.

For the most part the Weaver Birds suspend their nests to the ends of twigs, small branches, drooping parasites, palm-leaves, or reeds, and many species always hang their nests over water, and at no very great height above its surface. The object of this curious locality is evidently that the eggs and young should be saved from the innumerable monkeys that swarm in the forests, and whose filching paws would rob many a poor bird of its young brood. As, however, the branches are very slender, the weight of the monkey, however small the animal may be, is more than sufficient to immerse the would-be thief in the water, and so to put a stop to his marauding propensities.

Sawbill Humming-Bird   Brazilian Wood Nymph
White Sided Hill Star

Snakes, too, which are also inveterate nest-robbers, some of them living almost exclusively on young birds and eggs, are effectually debarred from entering the nests, so that the parent birds need not trouble themselves about either foe. Although they may repose in perfect safety, undismayed by the approach of either snake or monkey, they never can see one of their enemies without scolding at it, screaming hoarsely, shooting close to its body, and, if possible, indulging in a passing peck.

Such a scene is depicted in the illustration, where Weaver Birds of several species have united in their attacks upon a monkey that is endeavoring to rob a nest, and has met with a suitable fate.

In the right-hand upper corner of the illustration are seen the curious nests of the Mahali Weaver, accompanied by the birds themselves. The general shape of the nest is not unlike that of a Florence oil-flask, supposing the neck to be shortened and widened, the body to be lengthened, and the whole flask to be enlarged to treble its dimensions. Instead, however, of being smooth on the exterior, like the flask, it is intentionally made as rough as possible. The ends of all the grass-stalks, which are of very great thickness, project outward, and point toward the mouth of the nest, which hangs downward, so that they serve as eaves whereby the rain is thrown off the nest, and possibly serve also as a protection against foes, though the latter theory has not yet been corroborated by observation.

Just below the Mahali may be seen a number of roundish nests pendent from boughs. These are the homes of the Spotted Weaver, some having their entrance nearly at the bottom, and others toward the side. All, however, are constructed of similar material, and the different position of the mouth is evidently intended merely as an accommodation to circumstances.

In the left-hand lower corner is the long, retort-shaped nest of the pretty Yellow Weaver. The substance of which it is made is a very narrow, stiff, and elastic grass, scarcely larger than the ordinary twine used for tying up small parcels, and interwoven with a skill that seems far beyond the capabilities of a mere bird.

When viewed merely from the outside this nest looks as if it would be a very unsafe cradle, and would permit the young birds to

14

fall through the neck into the water. But if the hand be carefully introduced up the neck of one of these nests its admirable fitness for the nurture of the young birds is at once perceived, as well as the ingenious manner in which the interior is constructed. Just where the neck is united to the bulb a kind of wall or partition is made, about two inches in height, which runs completely across the bulb and effectually prevents the young birds from falling out.

Baya Sparrow

In the right-hand lower corner of the illustration is a nest of the pretty Taha Weaver, and hanging over the water near the bottom is the habitation of the Yellow-capped Weaver. The nest of this latter bird is notable for the extreme neatness and compactness of its structure, for it can endure avast amount of careless handling and still retain its beautiful contour. The whole structure is apparently composed of the same plant, namely, a kind of small reed, but the materials are taken from a different portion of the plant, according to the part of the nest for which they are required. The whole exterior, as well as the walls, are made of the reed-stems, woven very closely together, and being of no trifling thickness.

The interior, however, exhibits a lining of flat leaves, laid artistically over each other so as to form a soft, smooth resting-place, but not interlacing at all, being held in their place by their own elasticity. Their color is of a pale bluish gray, and the contrast which they present to the exterior is very strongly marked. In size the nest is about as large as an ordinary cocoa nut—not quite so long, though broader.

The Sociable Weaver bird, a native of Southern Africa, constructs a habitation in no wise inferior to those already mentioned. This wonderful specimen of bird architecture attracts the attention of the most unobservant traveler, being often large enough to shelter several persons. Though originally commenced by a single pair, it attains its enormous dimensions by the united labors of a community of birds, The first task of this Weaver Bird is to procure a quantity of a peculiar species of grass, which has a large, tough, and wiry blade. This grass they carry to some suitable tree, usually an acacia, the wood of which is hard and tough, and the branches consequently able to bear the great weight of the nests. Then, by means of weaving and plaiting the grass, they form a roof of some little size. Under this roof are placed a quantity of nests, increasing in number with each successive brood. They are set closely together, so that at last they look like a mass of grass pierced with numerous holes, and it is really wonderful that the birds should be able to find their way to their own particular homes.

Although the same nest-mass is occupied for several successive seasons, the birds refuse to brood in the same nests a second time, preferring to make a fresh domicile for each new brood. In consequence of this custom, when the birds have entirely filled the roof with their nests, they do not desert it, but enlarge the roof. Layer after layer is thus added, until the mass becomes of so enormous a size that travelers have mistaken these nests for the houses of human beings, and been grievously disappointed when they came near enough to detect their real character. There is a story of a Hottentot and a lion, which will give an idea of the dimensions of these nests. A Hottentot, who was engaged in some task, was suddenly surprised by a lion, and instinctively made for the nearest tree. Up the tree he sprang, and finding one of the branches occupied by the nest of the Sociable Weaver Bird, he took refuge behind the grassy mass, and was thus concealed from the pursuer. The lion, meantime, arrived at the foot of the tree, but could not see his intended prey. The unlucky Hottentot, however, peeped over the nest in order to see whether the coast was clear, and was spied by the lion, who made a dash at the tree. The man shrank back behind the nest, but his imprudent movement brought its own punishment.

Unable to ascend the tree, and at the same time unwilling to leave his prey, the lion sat down at the foot of the tree. Hour after hour the lion mounted guard over his prisoner, until thirst overpowered hunger, and the animal was forced reluctantly to quit his post and seek for water. The man then scrambled down the tree, and made the best of his way homeward, little the worse for his imprisonment except the fright, and a skin scorched by long exposure to the sun. The artist has introduced this little episode into the illustration, because it enables the reader to judge of the enormous size of the nest.

Season after season the Weaver Birds continue to add their nests, until at last the branch is unable to endure the weight, and comes crashing to the ground. This accident does not often occur during the breeding months, but mostly takes place during the rainy season, the dried grass absorbing so much moisture, that the weight becomes too great for the branch to bear.

The dimensions of some of these structures may be gathered from the fact, that there have been counted in one unfinished edifice, besides the deserted nests of previous seasons, no less than three hundred and twenty nests, each of which was occupied by a pair of birds engaged in bringing up a brood of young, four or five in number.

Crested Cassique   Baltimore Oriole

There are many pensile builders among American birds, and chief among them are the exquisite little humming-birds. When their nests are suspended from leaves, as is most commonly the case, some very tenacious substance must be employed to fasten them securely. This is found in the webs of various spiders, some of which are of wonderful strength and elasticity, and from them the birds can procure the long elastic threads with which the materials of the nest can be tied together, or the soft felt-like substances with which the moss, bark, and fibers can be interwoven, so as to form a firm and wet-resisting mass.

Fairy Martin   Pied Grallina

The Little Hermit is the name given to a beautiful species of humming-bird whose habitation is a curiously formed nest, funnel-shaped, and attached to the end of some drooping leaf. It is composed of the silky fibers of plants, the cotton-like down of seed vessels, and some other substance, which is supposed to be fungus, and is of a woolly texture. All these materials are interwoven with spider's-web, by means of which the nest is attached to the leaf at the end of which it swings.

Oven Bird

The Sawbill humming-bird, so called because its slender bill is notched in a saw-like fashion, makes its nest of fine vegetable fibers, woven together so as to look like an open net-work purse, the outer walls being so loosely made as to permit the eggs and lining to be visible. Leaves, mosses, and lichens are also woven into the nest, and are packed rather tightly under the eggs. The edge, however, is always left loose. The nest is suspended at the end of some leaf, usually that of the palm.

The Brazilian Wood Nymph is perhaps more persecuted than any other species of hummingbird, its singular beauty causing its plumage to be sought after. The feather on the crown of the head and front of the throat are of the most lovely azure, and are largely used by the inmates of several convents at Rio Janeiro for the purpose of being made into the beautiful feather flowers which the nuns manufacture so skillfully. Thousands of these birds are slaughtered merely for the crest and gorget, but so prolific are they, and so ingeniously do they hide their nests, that the persecution of many years has scarcely diminished their numbers. Moreover, fortunately for the preservation of the species, the colors of the female are so dull and sober that her feathers are of no value, and she is allowed to escape the fate that befalls the more brightly colored male. It is a lively little bird, and when alarmed utters a hurried cry, sounding like the word, "Pip, pip, pip," very sharply pronounced. The nest of the Brazilian Wood Nymph is exceedingly pretty, and is hung to the tip of some delicate twig, generally that of one of the creeping plants which trail their long stems so luxuriantly over the branches of the great forest trees. The walls of the nest are made of vegetable fibers, generally taken from the fruit of some palm, and upon the outside are fastened many patches of flat lichen, so that the whole nest, which is very long in proportion to its width, may easily escape detection.

The White-sided Hill Star is a native of the Andes, inhabiting a zone of very great elevation, seldom being seen less than ten thousand feet above the level of the sea. With the exception of a bright emerald-green gorget, it is rather a dull-colored bird, the prevailing hue being brown. The nest is shaped something like a hammock, and is fastened to the side of a rock; being suspended by one side so as to leave the remainder free. As is the case with the generality of humming-birds' nests, cobwebs are employed for the purpose of fastening the structure to the object to which it hangs. The materials of which the nest is made are chiefly down, and feathers, the feathers being profusely stuck on the outside.

The appearance and habits of the Baltimore Oriole, as well as the structure of its nest, may be familiar to many of our readers, since its residence is not confined to any particular locality. A good idea of the general shape of the nest may be formed from the illustration. The materials for it, however, are extremely variable, the bird having a natural genius for modification, and being always ready to take advantage of any new discovery in architecture.

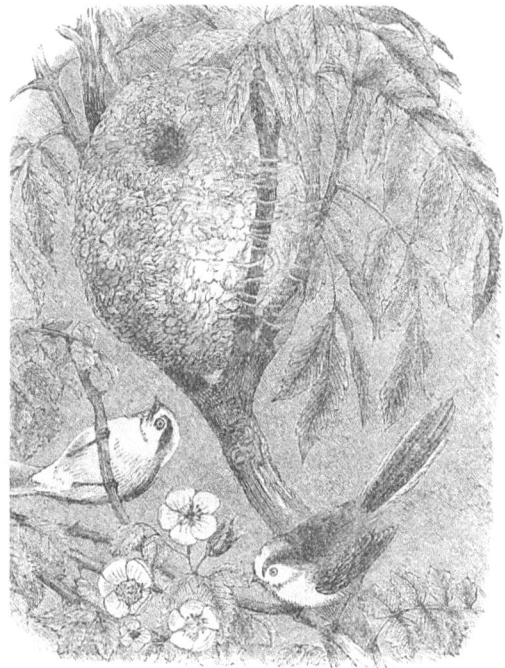

The Long Tailed Titmouse

Near the nest of the Baltimore Oriole is represented a very curious structure swaying in the wind, long, purse-like, and having the entrance near the top. This is the nest of the Crested Cassique, or Crested Oriole, and the bird itself is seen clinging to the lower part of the nest. A handsome creature is this bird, the greater part of the body being rich chocolate, the wings dark green, and the outer tail-feathers bright yellow, this color being displayed conspicuously as the bird flies, particularly when it makes a sharp turn in the air and is obliged to spread its tail-feathers rapidly. The beak of this species is very remarkable, being of a green color, and extending far up the forehead. The head is adorned with a long-point eel crest, from which its popular name of Crested Oriole is derived. Its nest is of great length, and, as may be seen by the illustration, has the entrance like that of a pocket. The opening is rather small when compared with the size of the nest itself, and the bird always dives head foremost into its home, its yelllow tail flashing a last golden gleam before it disappears. The nest is strongly built, and the materials are rather coarse, not in the least resembling the delicate and neatly rounded fibers of which many of the Weaver nests are made. These nests often exceed a yard in length, and, owing to their great size, are very conspicuous, as the wind sways them backward and forward from the bough.

In Ceylon is found the Baya Sparrow, whose nest is as remarkable as any specimen that has yet been mentioned. As may be seen by the illustration, these domicile's are variable in shape, and hang close to each other; indeed the birds are very sociable in all their manners, and fly about in great numbers, flocks of thousands flitting among the branches and displaying their pretty plumage to the sun. They have no Song, and can only chirp in a monotonous manner, but the want of song finds its compensation in the brilliancy of the plumage, which is mostly bright yellow. They are particularly fond of the acacias and date trees, and choose the branches of those trees for the suspension of their nests. Sometimes the nest is only made for incubation, sometimes it is intended merely as an arbor in which the male sits while the female incubates her eggs, and sometimes it consists of the nest and arbor united, producing a most curious effect.

Among the building birds there is one species which is preeminently superior. Not only is there no equal, but there is no second. This is the Oven Bird, which derives its name from the shape and material of its nest. It is about as large as a lark, and is a bold-looking bird, rather slenderly built, and standing very upright.

Its color is warm brown. It is very active, running and walking very fast, and is much on the wing, though its flights are not of long duration, consisting chiefly of short flittings from bush to bush in search of insects. It generally haunts the banks of South American rivers, and is a fearless little creature, not being alarmed even at the presence of man. The chief interest of this bird centers in its nest, which is a truly remarkable example of bird architecture. The material from which it is made is principally mud or clay obtained from the river banks, but it is strengthened and stiffened by the admixture of grass and various vegetable fibers. The heat of the sun is sufficient to harden it, and when it has been thoroughly dried, it is so strong that it seems more like the handiwork of some novice at pottery than a veritable nest constructed by a bird, the fierce heat of the tropical sun baking the clay nearly as hard as brick. The ordinary shape of the nest is domed and rounded, and has the entrance in the side. Its walls are fully an inch in thickness, and it looks strong enough to bear rolling about on the ground. The bird is not very particular as to the locality of its nest, sometimes building it on a branch of a tree, sometimes on a beam in an outhouse, and now and then on the top of palings, generally, however, it is built in the bushes, but without any attempt at concealment. Owing to its dimensions and shape the nest is extremely conspicuous, and the utter indifference of the bird on this subject is not the least curious part of its history. If one of the nests be carefully divided, the interior will be found even more curious than the outside. Crossing the nest from side to side is a partition made of the same materials as the outer shell, and reaching nearly to the top of the dome, thus dividing it into two chambers, and also strengthening the whole structure. The inner chamber is devoted to the work of incubation, and within it is a soft bed of feathers upon which the eggs are laid.

Although in the shape of its nest the Pied Grallina does not resemble the Oven Bird, the materials with which it is constructed are almost identical. Like the Oven Bird, also, it makes no attempt to conceal its nest, but places it quite conspicuously on a branch. It is almost invariably built on a bough which overhangs the water; and notwithstanding its weight and size; it is so firmly secured that there is no fear lest it should overbalance itself. The walls of the edifice are very thick and solid, and it looks like an exceedingly rude and ill-baked earthenware vessel, just such an one, indeed, as Robinson Crusoe manufactured on his island.

The Bower Bird

The curious flask-shaped nests which are seen in the illustration are built wholly of clay and mud, and are made by a beautiful little Australian bird, named the Fairy Martin, which is closely allied, as its generic name signifies, to the swallows and martins of Great Britain. These remarkable nests are generally to be found upon rocks, and are close to rivers, though occasionally the bird chooses another locality. The shape of the nests always resembles that of a flask or retort, and their size is extremely variable, the length of the necks being, from seven to ten inches, and the diameter of the bulb varying from four to seven inches. It is stated that each nest is the joint work of several birds, six or seven being sometimes employed upon one nest, one sitting in the interior, as chief architect, arranging and smoothing the material, while the others go off in search of mud and clay, which they knead well in their mouths before applying it to the nest.

Nest of the Chaffinch

As is generally the case with clay which is thus kneaded, it becomes very hard when baked in the sun, but, at the same time, is rather slow in drying. When the weather is dry the bird can only work in the mornings and evenings, because the heat of the sunbeams soon renders the clay too stiff to be worked by the delicate beaks of the birds, and therefore in the middle of the day the Fairy Martins cease from their architectural labors and do nothing but chase flies. During wet weather, however, when no flies are abroad, and the air is full of moisture, the birds work continually at their nests, and soon complete their labors. The exterior of the nest is quite as rough as that of the common English martin, but in the interior it is beautifully smooth.

The Long-tailed Titmouse is a pretty little bird, very plentiful in England, and owing to its habit of associating in little flocks of ten or twelve in number, and the exceeding restlessness of its character, is very familiar to all observers of nature. These flocks generally consist of the parent and their offspring, for the little creature is exceedingly prolific, laying a vast quantity of tiny eggs in its warm nest, and rearing most of the young to maturity. This is a bird which ought to be cherished by all possessors of fields or gardens, for there is scarcely a more determined enemy to the many noxious insects which destroy the fruits, vegetables, and flowers. A Very few are sufficiently early risers to learn the habits of the Long-tailed Titmouse by personal observation. At an early hour in the morning it allows itself to be watched without showing fear of diffidence. But A later in the day it is very timid. The shape of its nest is usually oval, and has an aperture at one side, near the top, through which the birds can pass. The materials of which the nest is made are mosses of various kinds, wool, hair, and similar substances, woven with great firmness. It is remarkable that in the construction of this nest, which requires peculiar solidity, the Long-tailed Titmouse uses materials like those which are employed by the humming-birds, and binds its nest together with the webs of spiders, and the silken hammocks of various caterpillars. The exterior of the nest is covered with lichens, so that the whole edifice looks very much like a natural excrescence upon the tree or bush in which it is placed. Sometimes the form of the nest is rather different from that which has been mentioned, and. the structure is flask-shaped. Now and then a nest is found in which there are two openings, one near the top in the usual position, and the other on the opposite side and near the bottom. The presence of one or two apertures is probably influenced by the position of the nest and the climate of the locality. If the finger be introduced into the aperture a charmingly soft and warm bed of downy feathers is felt, in which, rather than on which, the numerous eggs repose.

Nest of Goldfinch

Perhaps the whole range of ornithology does not produce a more singular phenomenon than the fact of a bird building a house merely for amusement, and decorating it with brilliant objects as if to mark its destination. Such a proceeding marks a great progress in civilization, and it is somewhat startling to find that in this we have long been anticipated by a bird which was unknown until within the last few years.

Golden Orioles and Nest

The ball-room or "bower" which the Bower bird of Australia builds is a very remarkable erection. Its general form may be seen by reference to the illustration, but the method by which it is constructed can only be learned by watching the feathered architect at work. It begins by weaving a tolerably firm platform of Small twigs, which look as if the bird had been trying to make a door-mat and had nearly succeeded. It then seeks for some long and rather slender twigs and pushes their bases into the platform, working them tightly into its substance, and giving them such an inward inclination that their tips cross each other and form a simple arch. As the twigs are set along the platform on both sides the bird gradually makes an arched alley, extending variably both in length and height. When the bower is completed one may well ask the use to which it can be put. It is not a nest, nor has the real nest of this bird been yet discovered. It serves as an assembly-room, in which a number of birds take their amusement, running through it, and chasing one another in a very sportive fashion. Why these birds should trouble themselves to make this bower is a problem as yet unsolved. Had the structure served in any way as a protection from the weather, there would have been a self-evident reason for its existence, but the arching twigs are put together so loosely that they can not protect the birds from wind or rain. Whatever may be the object of the bower, the birds are so fond of it that they resort to it during many hours of the day, and a good bower is seldom left without a temporary occupant.

Ornament is also employed by the Bower Bird, both entrances of the bower being decorated with bright and shining objects. The bird is not in the least fastidious about the articles with which it decorates its bower, provided only that they shine and are conspicuous. Scraps of colored ribbon, shells, bits of paper, teeth, bones, broken glass and china, feathers, and similar articles, are in great request, and such objects as a lady's thimble, a tobacco-pipe, and a tomahawk have been found near one of their bowers. Indeed, whenever the natives lose any small and tolerably portable object they always search the bowers of the neighborhood, and frequently find that the missing article is doing duty as decoration to the edifice.

A vast proportion of the feathered tribes select branches of trees or shrubs as the site of their habitation. Among the most conspicuous of all ordinary branch nests are those which are made by the Rooks and the Crows. They are large, dark, and are placed upon the topmost boughs of the tree, so that they can be seen at a considerable distance. Their position is evidently intended as a safeguard against the attacks of various enemies, among which the bird-nesting boy is preeminently the most dangerous. But the birds themselves seem to have a wonderful knack of choosing those trees which are most difficult of ascent; and place their nests on the extremities of the longest and most slender branches, so as often to baffle the most skillful efforts of their enemies.

Nest of the Reed Warbler

The Chaffinch, on the other hand, takes a very different method to protect its home. The nest is never easily seen, and its discovery requires a special training of the eye. This bird likes to find the fork of a tree, where several branches are thrown out from one spot, and so as to form a sort of cup in which the nest can lie. Within the forked branches the Chaffinch constructs its nest, chiefly of wool, matted together so as to form a kind of loose felt, with which are woven delicate mosses, spider-webs, cottony down, and lichens. The mosses and lichens are stuck most ingeniously upon the outside of the nest, and have the effect of making it look exactly like a natural excrescence from the tree in which it is placed. This pretty nest is generally deep in proportion to its width, and is lined with hairs, arranged in a most methodical manner, so as to form a cup for the eggs. The hair of the cow is much used by the Chaffinch, and it may be seen collecting its stock in the fields, searching in the crevices of trees and posts, against which the cattle are accustomed to rub themselves. The nest is strong, and owing to the nature of the materials, is very elastic, returning to its original state even after severe pressure.

Water Hen and Nest

The nest of the Goldfinch is constructed much like that of the Chaffinch, excepting that it is shallower, and the lichens and moss of which it is partly made are not stuck on the outside, but are woven so deeply into the walls that the whole surface is quite smooth. The position of the two nests, however, is very different. Instead of choosing the forks of a bough, the Goldfinch likes to make its nest near the end of a horizontal branch, so that it waves about and dances up and down as the branch is swayed by the wind. It might be thought that the eggs would be shaken out by a tolerably sharp breeze, and such would indeed be the case, were they not kept in their place by the form of the nest. On examination, it will be seen to have the edge thickened and slightly turned inward, so that when the nest is tilted on one side by the swaying of the bough the eggs are still retained within. The Goldfinch's nest is usually lined with vegetable down, which it uses in preference to any other material. On this soft bed reposes five pretty eggs, white, tinged with blue, and diversified with small grayish-purple spots. Altogether, it is hardly possible to find a more beautiful group than is made by a pair of Goldfinches, their nest, and eggs.

The Golden Oriole is rarely seen in England; but in the warmer parts of the continent it is plentiful, and in Italy it is highly esteemed by epicures, toward the middle of autumn, when it has become fat and plump by the free use of fruit. The nest of the Golden Oriole is always placed near the extremity of a branch, and in some cases is so constructed that it almost deserves to be ranked among the pensiles. It is always a pretty nest, and the illustration conveys a good idea of its general form. It is always more or less cup-like in shape, but the comparative depth of the cup is very variable, as in some cases it is scarcely deeper in proportion than that of the Goldfinch, and rather saucer-shaped, while in others the depth even exceeds the width. Perhaps the nest may be altered in shape after the female begins to deposit her eggs, as is known to be the case with many birds, the additions being always made to the margin. The object for deepening the nest may probably be traced to the weather which happens to prevail. If the winds be light, it may remain in its flat and saucer-like form without endangering the safety of the eggs; but if the season should be inclement and tempestuous, a deeper nest is needed in order to prevent the eggs or young from being flung out of their home.

Fiery Topaz and Hermit

The body of the nest is formed chiefly of vegetable substances, usually the stems of different grasses, which are interwoven with wool, and thus made into a tolerably strong fabric. The female bird is said to be very affectionate, and to sit so closely on her nest that she will almost suffer the hand to be laid upon her before she will leave her post. In the illustration the female bird is standing upright on the branch, and looking upward, while the male is bending over the bough, and peering downward, as if at some fancied foe.

34

Edible Swallow

The nest of the Water Hen is always placed near the water, though the bird seems very indifferent about the precise locality. Sometimes it is made on the ground, among sedges and rushes, and sometimes on a branch which overhangs the water. The nest is large and rudely made, and when it is placed on a bough, the twigs of the same branch often dip into the water, and the nest looks like a bunch of weeds other debris that have floated down the stream and been arrested by the branch. The similitude is increased by a curious habit of the bird. When she leaves her nest, she pulls over her eggs a quantity of the same substances as those which form the materials of the nest, so that they are completely hidden from sight, and the form of the nest quite obscured. When the nest is found with the eggs exposed, this apparent neglect is always caused by the frightened bird clashing off at the approach of an intruder, and having no time to cover them properly. The young of this bird are the oddest little beings imaginable, looking like spherical puffs of black down rather than birds. They take to the water at once, and if one can manage to watch the mother and her little family, he will see one of the quaintest and prettiest groups in the World. The little black balls swim about quite at their ease, keeping within a short distance of their parent, and traversing the water with wonderful rapidity.

The remarkably beautiful nest of the Reed Warbler, a British bird, is not often found on account of the localities where it is placed. This pretty little architect loves a patch of marshy land, almost wholly covered with stagnant water, and full of the reeds among which its home is made—not an agreeable place of investigation to the pedestrian. The nest is supported between three or four reeds, as is shown in the illustration, and is remarkably deep in proportion to its width. The object of this depth is evident. To bend as a reed before the wind is a proverbial saying, and any one who has seen a large mass of reeds on a stormy day must have been impressed with their graceful curves. A nest, therefore, which rests on such pliant supports must be thrown out of its perpendicular by every breath of wind, and unless it were very deep the eggs would be flung out. The great depth, however, of the nest, counteracts the deflection of the reeds, and, however fiercely the storm may rage, the Reed Warbler sits securely in her nest, even though it be sometimes nearly bowed to the surface of the water. The materials of the nest are generally taken from the immediate neighborhood, the body of it being composed of broken rushes and moss bound together with reed leaves, and the lining made almost wholly of cow's hair. In the illustration the nest is represented as it appears during a rather smart breeze. The reeds are all bowed down by the force of the wind, and the nest is leaning so much to one side, that its contents would be flung into the water were it of the ordinary cup-shaped form. The tiny inmates, however, are perfectly secure in their home, and crouch in the bottom of the nest, so that there is no fear that they may be thrown out. The parent birds are busily attending on their little family, one having just brought an insect which all the gaping mouths are eager to devour, while the other is setting off in its turn to perform the like office.

Nightengale

In an illustration are shown the nests of two species of Humming-bird. The oddly-shaped nest which occupies the upper part of the drawing is made by the Fiery Topaz, one of the most magnificent of these lovely birds. The body is fiery scarlet, the head velvet-black, the throat glittering emerald, with a patch of crimson in the center, the lower part of the back is also green, and, the long, slender, crossed feathers of the tail are purple with a green gloss. So magnificent a bird can have but few rivals, and there is only one species that even approaches it in beauty. This is the Crimson Topaz, a bird which is nearly allied to it, and which much resembles it in general coloring. Curiously enough, although it is bedecked with resplendent hues, which seem to need the presence of daylight, and to be made expressly for the purpose of reflecting the brightest beams of the sun, yet the lovely bird is one of the night-wanderers, being seldom seen as long as the sun is above the horizon, and preferring to seek its food while the world is shrouded in darkness.

The Albatross

The nest which is built by the Fiery Topaz is really a wonderful structure. Its shape is remarkable, and is well shown in the illustration. It is fastened to the branch with extreme care, as is clearly necessary from its general form. The most curious point

38

about the nest is, however, the material of which it is made. When it was first discovered no one knew how the bird could have built so strange a structure. It looked as if it were made of very coarse buff leather, and was so similar in hue to the branches that surrounded it, that it seemed more like a natural excrescence than a birds-nest. The reason for this similitude was simple enough. It was made of a natural excrescence, and therefore resembled one.

When the Fiery Topaz wishes to build a nest, it goes off to the trees, and searches for a peculiar kind of fungus, and with this singular material it makes its home. It is tough, leathery, thick, and soft, and in some curious manner the bird contrives to mold the apparently intractable substance into the shape which is represented in the illustration.

The lower figure in the illustration represents the net of another species of Humming-bird, belonging to the pretty little group popularly called Hermits, and which may be recognized by the peculiar shape of the tail. All the Hermits are remarkable for the beauty of their homes. The nest of this species is always long and funnel-shaped, and is hung either to a leaf or a delicate twig of a tree.

There is a remarkable species of bird, to which is given the popular name of Edible, or Esculent Swallow, not because it is itself edible, but because its nest is eaten in some countries. We have heard of birds-nest soup, and some may possibly have imagined that the nests in question are made of the ordinary vegetable substances, such as moss, leaves, and twigs. In reality they are formed of some gelatinous substance, though its true nature is still uncertain, no one precisely knowing whether it is of animal or vegetable origin. Some persons have thought that the material is fish spawn, which the bird fetches from the sea, others have supposed it to be a kind of seaweed, which is dissolved in the bird's crop and then disgorged; while others believe that it is secreted by certain glands in the throat, and proceeds entirely from the body of the architect. When first made these nests are very white and delicate in their aspect, and in that condition are extremely valuable, being sold at an extravagant price to the Chinese. They soon darken by use and exposure, and are not fit for the purposes of the table until they have been cleaned and bleached. These nests are found in Borneo, Java, etc., and are extremely local, being confined to certain spots. The birds always choose the sides of deep cavernous precipices, so that the task of obtaining the nests is extremely dangerous. They are attached to the perpendicular rocks much as the ordinary mud-built swallow nests, and are generally arranged in horizontal layers. The caverns in which the nests are placed are extremely valuable, and are preserved with jealous care from any intruder. On the outside the nests have a shelly appearance, being arranged in regular layers, with distinct edges. The material is so translucent that when placed on printed paper and held to the light the capital letters can be plainly read through its substance. A glance at the interior shows at once the mode of its construction.

It is made of innumerable glutinous threads, which have been drawn irregularly across each other, and have hardened by exposure to the air into a material which much resembles isinglass. The nests, when used as an article of food, are steeped in hot water for a considerable time. When they soften into a gelatinous mass, which forms the basis of a fashionable soup, not unlike turtle soup. The Chinese value this soup highly, thinking that it possesses great power of restoring lost strength. It is, however, far too costly to be obtained by any but the rich.

The nest of the Nightingale is always set very near the ground, and in most cases. is scarcely raised more than a few inches above the soil. In one sense it is not a pretty nest, and its apparent roughness of construction is probably intended to make it less conspicuous. The discovery of a Nightingale's nest is not an easy task, unless the eye be directed to the spot by watching the movements of the bird. It is always most carefully concealed under growing foliage, and is composed of grass, straw, little sticks, and dried leaves, all jumbled together with such "artless art" that even when a nest is seen its real nature often escapes detection. In consequence of the position which they occupy, the materials look like a mass of loose debris that has been blown by wind and arrested by the foliage among which it has been lodged. The eggs are equally inconspicuous, being dull olive-brown, without a spot or streak. After they are laid, the lively song of the Nightingale becomes less and less frequent, while after the young are hatched the bird is silent until the next season.

The Wandering Albatros, the giant of the petrel tribe, makes its nest after a peculiar fashion. It chooses the summit of lofty precipices near the sea, and its nest may be found plentifully in the islands of the Southern Atlantic Ocean. The Albatros is lord of the country, and no other living being seems to intrude upon its nesting-place. So completely do the birds feel themselves masters of the situation, that if a human being penetrates to their haunts they quietly move about as if he were non-existent, and do not appear to take the least notice of him. On such elevated positions the cold is necessarily intense, but the Albatros cares not for the cold, and brings up its white-coated young in a temperature that few human beings would care to endure. The Albatros lays only a single egg, and no particular bed seems necessary for it. The mother bird simply deposits it on the bare ground, and then scrapes earth around it, so as to form a small circular wall, as may be seen by reference to the illustration.

The Coot, sometimes called the Bald Coot, on account of the horny plate on its forehead, which is pink during the breeding season and white during the rest of the year, forms an ingenious structure for its home. It's favorite nesting-places are little islands on which the grass grows rankly. Failing them it will make its nest among reeds and rushes, binding and twisting them together until they are firm enough to support the weight of the nest, the bird, and the many eggs. The nest contains a great number of eggs, seldom less than seven, and sometimes twelve or fourteen. They are whitish, and profusely spotted with irregular brown marks. In the illustration the haunts of the Coot are well represented. In the foreground is one of the grass tussocks, of which a pair of Coots have taken possession, and in which the young are seen under the protection of their parents. Similar tussocks protrude from the shallow water, and from one of them the mother Coot is issuing, followed by her young brood. In the back-ground are seen a pair of swans, one of which is bearing her young on her back, according to the custom of her kind.

The Coot

Mammals and Insects Part 1

Mouse Nest in a Bottle

THERE are very few animals among the Mammalia who venture to exert their skill upon aerial architecture. Consequently the Harvest Mouse, found in many parts of England, is regarded with special interest ; and this not only because its home is suspended above the ground in such a manner as to entitle it to the name of a true pensile nest, but also on account of its intrinsic beauty and elegance. The nest is generally hung to several stout grass-stems; sometimes it is fastened to wheat straws; and occasionally it is found suspended to the head of a thistle. It is a very beautiful structure, being made of very narrow grasses, and woven so carefully as to form a hollow globe, rather larger than a cricket-ball, and very nearly as round. The Harvest Mouse is an elegant little creature, so tiny that, when full-grown, it weighs scarcely more than the sixth of an ounce, and we can not but wonder how it contrives to form so complicated an object as a hollow sphere with thin walls. The walls are so thin that an object inside the nest can be easily seen from any part of the exterior; there is no opening whatever, and

Harvest Mouse

when the young are in the nest they are packed so tightly that their bodies press against the wall in every direction. As there is no defined opening, and as the walls are so loosely woven, it is probable that the mother is able to push her way between the meshes, and so to arrange or feed her young. The position of the nest, which is always at some little height, presupposes a climbing power in the architect. All mice and rats are good climbers, but the Harvest Mouse is especially well fitted for climbing, inasmuch as its long and flexible toes can firmly grasp the grass stem, and its long slender tail aids it materially in sustaining itself. As the food of the Harvest Mouse consists greatly of insects, flies being especial favorites, it is evident that great agility is needed. In order to show the active character of the quadruped, one of the harvest mice is represented in the engraving as climbing toward a fly, upon which it is about to pounce. In such circumstances its leap is remarkably swift, and its aim as accurate as that of a swallow. In the airy cradle of the Harvest Mouse may sometimes be seen as many as eight young mice, all packed together like herrings in a barrel.

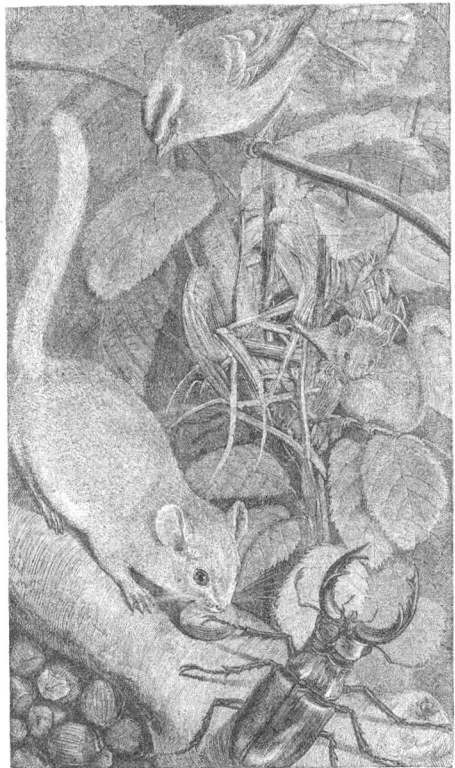

Dormouse and Nest

The Common Mouse, also, is a notable little house-builder, making nests out of various materials, and placing them oftentimes in very odd places, as the following instances will show : At the end of autumn a number of flower-pots had been set aside in a shed, in waiting for the coming spring. Toward the middle of winter the shed was cleared out and the flower-pots removed. While carrying them out of the shed the owner was rather surprised to find a round hole in the mould, and examined it closely. In the hole was seen, not a plant, but the tail of a mouse, which leaped from the pot as soon as it was set down. Presently another mouse followed from the same aperture, showing that a nest lay beneath the soil. On removing the earth a neat and comfortable nest was found, made chiefly of straw and paper, the entrance to which was the hole through which the inmates had fled. The most curious point in connection with this nest was, that although the earth in the pot seemed to be intact except for the round hole, which might have been made by a stick, none was found within it: The ingenious little architects had been clever enough to scoop out the whole of the earth and to carry it away, so as to form a cavity for the reception of their nest. They, did not completely empty the pot, as if knowing by instinct that their habitation would be betrayed, but allowed a slight covering of earth to remain upon their nest. A number of empty bottles had been stowed away upon a shelf, and among them was found one which was tenanted by a mouse. The little creature had considered that the bottle would afford a suitable home for her young, and had therefore conveyed into it a quantity of bedding which she made into a nest. The bottle was filled with the nest, and the eccentric architect had taken the precaution to leave a round hole corresponding to the neck of the bottle. In this remarkable domicile the young were placed ; and it is a fact worthy of notice that no attempt had been made to shut out the light. Nothing would have been easier than to have formed the cavity at the under-side, so that the soft materials of the nest would exclude the light; but the mouse had simply formed a comfortable hollow for her young, and therein she had placed them. It is therefore evident that the mouse has no fear of light, but that it only chooses darkness as a means of safety for its young. The rapidity with which the mouse can make a nest is somewhat surprising. Some few years ago, in a farmer's house, a loaf of newly-baked bread was placed upon a shelf, according to custom. Next day a hole was observed in the loaf; and when it was cut open a mouse and her nest was discovered within, the latter having been made of paper. On examination, the material of the habitation was found to have been obtained from a copy-book, which had been torn into shreds and arranged into the form of a nest. Within this curious home were nine new-born mice. Thus in the space of thirty-six hours, at most, the loaf must have cooled, the interior been excavated, the book found and cut into suitable pieces, the nest made, and the young brought into the world. Surely it is no wonder that mice are so plentiful, or that their many enemies fail to exterminate them.

When in a state of liberty, and able to work in its own manner, the Dormouse is an admirable nest-maker. As it passes the day in sleep, it must needs have some retired domicile in which it can be hidden from the many enemies which might attack a sleeping animal. One of these nests is depicted in the illustration, being situated in a hedge about four feet from the ground, and is placed in the forking of a branch, the smaller twigs of which form a kind of palisade round it. The substances of which it is composed are of two kinds; namely, grass-blades and leaves of trees. Two or three kinds of grass are used, the greater part being the well-known sword-grass, whose sharp edges cut the fingers of a careless handler. The blades are twisted round the twigs and through the interstices, until they form a hollow nest, rather oval in shape. Toward the bottom the finer sorts of grass are used, as well as some stems of delicate climbing weeds, which are no larger than ordinary thread, and which serve to bind the mass together. Interwoven with the grass are leaves, which fill up the interstices. The entrance to the nest is so ingeniously concealed that to find it is not a very easy matter, even when its precise position is known; and in order to show the manner in which it is constructed, one of the Dormice is represented in the act of drawing aside the grass-blades that conceal it. The pendent pieces of grass that are being held aside by the little paw are so fixed, that when released from pressure they spring back over the aperture and conceal it in a very effectual manner. Such a nest is usually about six inches in length and three in width. Although the Dormouse uses this aerial house as a residence, it does not make use of it as a granary. Like many other hibernating animals, it collects a store of winter food, which generally consists of nuts, grain, and similar substances. These treasures are carefully hidden away in the vicinity of the nest, and in the illustration the animal is shown as eating a nut which it has taken from one of its storehouses beneath the thick branch.

The Stag Beetle and the Golden-crested Wren have been introduced into the illustration to show the comparative size of the animals.

Nest of Apoica

It is hardly possible to overrate the wonderful varieties of form that are assumed by the nests of insects—varieties so bold and so startling that few would believe in the possibility of their existence without ocular demonstration. No rule seems to be observed in them; at all events no rule has as yet been discovered by which their formation is guided; neither has any conjecture been formed as to the reason for the remarkable forms which they assume. In the British Museum there is a splendid collection of curious nests, but, none perhaps. which awakens more surprise and admiration than the wonderful group represented in the accompanying illustration. Although the seven nests were not all found adhering to a single, branch—being placed near each other only to allow of easy comparison—they were all made by an insect bearing the somewhat scientific name of Apoica. This insect, although by no means a handsome creature, well deserves its scientific title: By referring to the illustration it will be seen that the nests are by no means uniform in size or shape. The larger one, which occupies the centre, rather exceeds ten inches in diameter, while the small nest at the end of the same branch is scarcely half as wide, and the others are of all the intermediate sizes. In shape, too, they differ, some being perfectly hexagonal, others partly so, while others again are nearly circular, though on a careful inspection they show faint traces of the hexagonal form. The upper surfaces are more or less convex, according to their size; this form being evidently intended for the purpose of making them water-proof. In fact, the nests somewhat resemble shallow basins with very thick sides, and bear an almost startling resemblance to the cap of a very large and well-shaped mushroom, the central specimen being so fungus-like in form that, if it were laid on the ground in a waste and moist spot, it would soon be picked up as a veritable mushroom. The color is in general a yellowish brown, although occasionally some nest boldly departs from the general uniformity, presenting a reddish surface, or even a white. All the nests are fixed in the same manner to a branch or twig passing through the upper surface. When the nest is increased in size the original support is often found to be too slight, and in that case others are added. The cells are arranged in the most systematic manner in rows which follow the exterior outline, and therefore take the shape of a hexagon. How the insect forms these wonderful cell-groups is an enigma to which not the least clew can be found. In proportion to the size of the architect they are simply enormous, and yet the sides and angles are as true and just as if they were single cells.

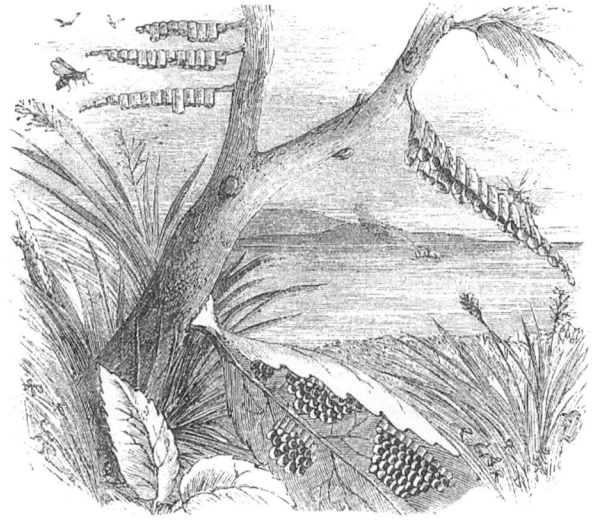

Nests of Icarias

Very curious nests are made by several species of an insect belonging to the genus Icaria. These nests, or rather these series of cells, are made after a singular fashion. First, the insect attaches to the branch a foot-stalk composed of the same material as that with which the cells are formed. This foot-stalk, although slender, is very hard, solid, and tough, and can uphold a considerable weight, as is necessary from the manner of constructing the nest. She then makes a cell after the ordinary wasp-fashion, attaching it to the foot-stalk with its mouth downward, and at first making it comparatively short. When the cell has nearly attained its due length a second is placed alongside the first, and a third is added in like manner, each being lengthened as required. As the cells at the base of the series are finished first it is evident that they gradually diminish toward the end, those at the extremity being often not one quarter so long as those at the base.

The common Hive Bee deserves our admiration on account of the wonderful manner in which it constructs its social home, and the method by which that home is regulated. But there is another insect, as well known by name, but with whose habits we are somewhat shy of attempting to become intimately familiar. This is the common Hornet, whose nest is almost invariably built in hollow trees, deserted outhouses, and places of a similar description.

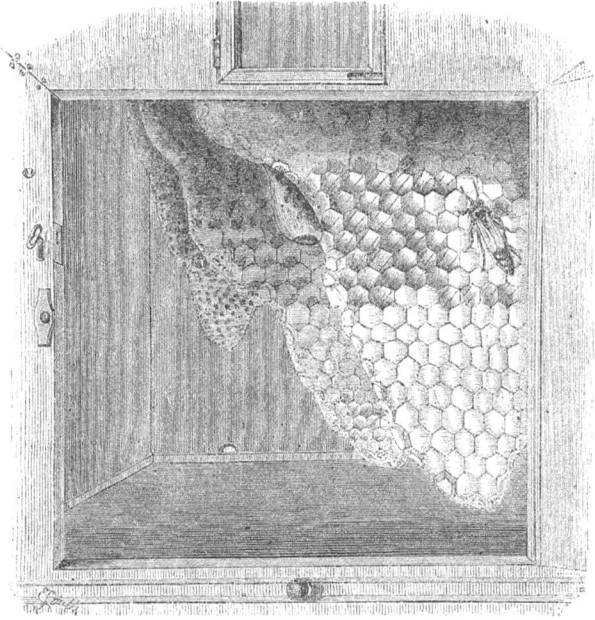

Hive of the Bee

Whenever the Hornet takes up its residence in an inhabited house, as is sometimes the case, the inmates are sure to be in arms against the insect, and with good reason. Its sting is exceedingly venomous, and it is popularly said that three hornets can kill a man. Moreover, the Hornet is an irascible insect, and given to assault those whom it fancies are approaching its nest with evil intentions. Consequently it is a matter of no slight difficulty to obtain a nest, or to watch the process of its construction. In the illustration is shown the exterior of a partially finished nest, and the manner in which the hornets enter at different parts. Hornets may be forced to build a much more beautiful nest than they ordinarily construct. One nest, when of moderate size, was removed by a naturalist from the head of a tree, and placed in a large glazed box, within which the hornets continued their labors, and a most beautiful nest was produced, symmetrical in shape and variegated with wonderfully rich colors. In order, however, to produce this result it is necessary to select the richest-colored woods, and place them where the insects shall be induced to use them in the construction of their nest.

Nest of the Hornet

In the collection of the British Museum may be seen a very remarkable nest, which is made by some species of wasp at present unknown, but which may appropriately be called the Mud Wasp. It was found in a Guianan forest suspended to a branch, which passed through a hole in the solid walls of the nest. Unfortunately, in its passage to England, it was broken and much damaged, but the fragments were collected and skillfully put together, and the nest restored to its original shape, with the exception of an aperture through which the interior may be seen. The material of which it is formed is mud, or clay, which is moulded by the insect until it has attained a wonderful tenacity and strength, and is rendered so plastic as to be worked nearly as neatly as the waxen bee-cell.

It is of rather a large size, measuring about thirteen inches in length, by nine in width, and filled with combs. A large quantity of clay is worked around the chosen branch, and made very strong, in order to sustain the heavy weight which will be suspended from it. This clay foundation is very hard, though brittle. One of the most remarkable points in the construction of this nest is the entrance. In pensile nests the insect usually forms the opening below, so that it may be sheltered from the wind and rain. Moreover, it is usually of small dimensions, evidently in order to prevent the inroads of parasitic insects and other foes, and to give the sentinels a small gateway to defend. But the particular wasp which built this remarkable nest seems to have set every rule at defiance, and to have shown an entire contempt of foes and indifference to rain. As may be seen by reference to the illustration, the entrance is extremely long, though not wide, and extends through nearly the length of the nest, so that the edges of the combs can be seen by looking into the aperture. The edges of the entrance are rounded, so that the outer edge is wider than the inner; but it is still sufficiently wide to allow the little finger of a man's hand to be passed into the interior; while its length is so great that forty or fifty insects might enter or leave the nest together.

The nest of the Pasteboard Wasp is suspended to a branch, which passes through a hole or ring so large that the structure is permitted to swing freely in the wind. The dimensions of the nest are variable, each one appearing to be capable of unlimited enlargement. The mode by which the wasps increase the size of their pensile home is equally simple and efficacious. When the number of the inhabitants becomes so large that a fresh series of cells is required, the insects enlarge their home with perfect ease, and at the same time without destroying its symmetry, a point which is often forgotten when human architects undertake the enlargement of some fine edifice. Taking the bottom of the nest as the starting-point, they build upon it a series of cells, taking care to add another row or two to the circumference, so as to increase the diameter in proportion to the length. They then add fresh material to the outer wall, which is lengthened so as to include the new tier of cells, and then the bottom is closed with a new floor, which in its turn will become the ceiling of the next tier of cells.

Nest of the Mud Wasp

An average nest is about one foot in length and of proportionate width; but now and then a positive giant of a nest is discovered where the colony has been undisturbed, and circumstances have been favorable to its increase. One of the largest, if not the very largest, of these pasteboard nests that has yet been discovered, was found in Ceylon, attached to the inside of a huge palm leaf, and was of the astonishing length of six feet.

Now, to form an idea of a nest six feet in length is not very easy. It is so huge as scarcely to be credited except from actual sight. We all know how conspicuous among ordinary men is one who measures six feet in height, and we shall form a better idea of the nest in question, if we reckon it to be equal in length to a "six-foot" man, and of course to occupy much more space on account of its bell-like shape.

Nest of the Pasteboard Wasp

The members of the genus Polistes are in the habit of building their cells in the open air, and leaving them without covering to defend them. The species which make the cells represented in the illustration is one of the most remarkable, both from the elegant form of the combs and the singular method of their attachment. Generally, the shape of the comb is nearly round, as is seen in the upper figure

Nests of Polistes

of the illustration. The cells are remarkable for their radiating form, the bases being a trifle smaller than the mouths, a peculiarity which would hardly be noticed in a single cell, but which produces the spreading outline when a number of them are massed together. Some of the cells are closed, indicating that the undeveloped insect is within. Now comes the curious part of the structure. The combs are not fastened directly to the branches, but are attached to foot-stalks which spring from their centre, and are firmly cemented upon the branch or twig. How wonderfully the insect must manage the comb so that it shall be balanced on this slender foot-stalk to preserve the equilibrium of even an empty comb would be difficult enough, but when the cells are filled with fat, heavy grubs the difficulty must be multiplied with every one. The foot-stalks are made of the same *papier-maché* like substance as the cells, only the layers are so tightly compressed together that they form a hard, solid mass, very much like the little pillars which support the different stories of an ordinary wasp's nest, but of much greater size. The position of the combs is extremely variable, some being nearly horizontal, and others perpendicular, as shown in the illustration. These came from Bareilly, in the East Indies.

Mammals and Insects Part II

The Water Spider

IN the tropical regions insect life flourishes as luxuriantly as the vegetation. There are insects that bite and insects that suck, insects that scratch and insects that sting, and many that are remarkable for giving out a most horrible odor. Some of them are cased in armor as hard as crab-shells, and will endure almost any amount of violence; while some are as round, as plump, as thin-skinned, and as juicy as over-ripe gooseberries, and collapse almost with a touch. There are great flying insects which always make for the light, and unless it is defended by glass will either put it out, or will singe their wings and spin about on the table in a manner that is by no means agreeable. The smaller insects get into the inkstand and fill it with their tiny carcasses, while others run over the paper and smear every letter as it is made. There are great centipedes, which are legitimate cause of dread, being armed with poison fangs scarcely less venomous than those of the viper. There are always plenty of scorpions; while the chief army is composed of cock-roaches, of dimensions, appetite, and odor such as we can hardly conceive in this favored land. As to the lizards, snakes, and other reptiles, they are so common as almost to escape attention. For a time these usurpers reign supreme. Now and then a few dozen are destroyed in a raid, or a person of sanguine temperament amuses his leisure hours, and improves his marksmanship by picking off the more prominent intruders with a saloon pistol; but the vacancies are soon filled up, and no permanent benefit is obtained. But there is one insect which, although often annoying, is also exceedingly useful; and its approach is welcomed by the inhabitants of tropical America, where it abounds. This is the Foraging Ant, which, though not more skillful than many other insects in constructing its home, is worthy of special notice. These ants sally forth in vast columns, at least a hundred yards in length, though not of very great width. When they make their appearance nothing withstands their assault; the inhabitants throw open every box and drawer in the house so as to allow the ants access into every crevice, and then retire from the premises. Presently the vanguard of the column approaches, a few scouts precede the general body, and seem to inspect the premises and ascertain whether they are worth a search. The long column then pours in and is soon dispersed over the house. The scene that then ensues is described as most singular. The ants penetrate into the corners, peer into each crevice, and speedily haul out any unfortunate creature that is lurking therein. Great cockroaches are dragged unwillingly away, being pulled in front by four or five ants; and pushed from behind by as many more. The rats and mice speedily succumb to the onslaught of their myriad foes, the snakes and lizards fare no better; and even the formidable weapons of the scorpion and centipede are overcome by their pertinacious foes. In a wonderfully short time the Foraging Ants have completed their work, the scene of turmoil gradually ceases, the scattered parties again form into line, and the procession moves out

Foraging Ants

of the house, carrying its spoils in triumph. The raid is most complete, and when the inhabitants return to the house they find every intruder gone, and to their great comfort are enabled to move about without treading on some unpleasant creature, and to put on their shoes without previously knocking them against the floor for the purpose of shaking out the scorpions and similar visitors. In the illustration a column of Foraging Ants is seen winding its way through a wood. Every one who is accustomed to the country takes particular care not to cross one of these columns. The Foraging Ants are tetchy creatures, and not having the least notion of fear, are terrible enemies even to human beings. If a man should happen to cross a column the ants immediately dash at him, running up his legs, biting fiercely with their powerful jaws, and injecting poison into the wound. The only plan of action in such a case is to run away at top speed until the main body are too far off to renew the attack, and then to destroy the ants that are already in action. This is no easy task, for the fierce little insects drive their hooked mandibles so deeply into the flesh that they are generally removed piecemeal, the head retaining its hold after the body has been pulled away, and the mandibles clasped so tightly that they must be pinched from the head and detached separately. There seems to be scarcely a creature which these insects will not attack, and they will even go out of their way to fall upon the nests of the large and formidable wasps of that country. For the thousand stings the ants care not a jot, but tear away the substance of their nest with their powerful jaws, penetrate into the interior, break, down the cells, and drag out the helpless young. Should they meet an adult wasp they fall upon it and cut it to pieces in a moment.

Nests of Termite

The African Termite erects nests of vast size and stone-like solidity. The history of this insect is complicated and full of incident, so that many pages might be occupied in giving an account of them, and yet the subject be not exhausted. The illustration, however, will afford some idea of the form and size of their habitations. A full-sized nest of the African Termite is a wonderful structure. Although made merely of clay, the walls are nearly as hard as stone, and hunters are accustomed to mount upon them for the purpose of looking out for game, and the wild buffalo has a similar habit, the structure being strong enough even to support the weight of so large an animal. The form of the nest is essentially conical, a large cone occupying the centre, and smaller cones being grouped round it like pinnacles round a Gothic spire. It is stated that nests have been seen that were full twenty feet in height, and that had a circumference of one hundred feet.

Fungus Ant

The accompanying illustration represents a most singular structure, which very little resembles an insect's nest. It might very well be taken for a sponge, looks much like a fungus, and has the appearance of an overgrown and partially decayed puff-ball. The real material, however, of which the nest is made, is formed of the short cottony fibres which fill the seed pods of the cotton tree. The fibre is so short that it is incapable of being woven into fabrics. The Fungus Ants, however, find it useful for their work, and contrive to weave it so dextrously that the individuality of the fibres is lost, and they are all made into a compact and uniform mass. The size of the nests varies, but is sometimes very considerable, a full-sized one, being often as large as a man's head. The ant itself is rather a curious little creature, dark in color, covered with many angular protuberances, and being remarkable for a couple of long, sharp spines that project from the thorax, one on either side.

On the right hand of the next illustration may be seen a large moth flying downward, and just above it are a couple of oval objects attached to a slender bough. This moth is that magnificent insect the Atlas Moth, and the oval objects are the cocoons which are spun by its larva. The Atlas Moth is a truly splendid insect. Creamy white, soft yellow, and pale brown are the chief tints it wears; but they are so beautifully blended, the plumage is of so downy a softness, and the expanse of wing is so great that the Atlas holds its own high rank even among the more vividly colored insects of its own country. There are many members of this genus scattered over the different parts of the earth, the finest and largest specimens being found between the tropics. In all the species the antennae of the males are remarkable for their beauty, being deeply feathered, and shaped something like a spearhead with a triangular blade, and in many examples there is a loose membranous talc like spot in the middle of the wing. The cocoons of the Atlas Moth are made of silken thread, much like that of the common silk-worm, the cocoon being large in proportion to the size of the moth, and the quantity of silk is necessarily very great. Although the thread is not so fine or glossy as that of the ordinary silk-worm, it is strong, smooth, and serviceable, and capable of being woven into useful fabrics.

House Builder Moth and Atlas Moth

The House-builder Moth is an insect which is common in many parts of the West Indies, in several places being so plentiful that the sight of its long pendent domiciles is any thing but pleasant to the proprietor of a garden. The reader will observe that in the illustration the nest is shown as depending from the caterpillar, part of which protrudes from its mouth and the other part is hidden. This attitude is given because it is that in which the insect is generally seen. Scraps of wood mixed with fragments of leaves are the materials which are used, and they are bound together very firmly by the silken threads with which so many caterpillars are endowed. There is a tolerable degree of elasticity about it, especially at the entrance, which is slightly expanded so as to assume an irregular funnel-like shape, and can be drawn together at will by means of the silken threads attached to its circumference. The caterpillar has thus two means of guarding itself from attacks. If it is still clinging to a branch, it can retreat into the house and press the mouth so firmly against the branch that it is closed effectively, just as a limpet shelters its soft body by pressing the top of the shell against the rock. Or, if detached, it can pull the lips together, and thus shut itself up in its strange house as completely as a box tortoise in its shell. The Oriental idea that feminine delicacy is only to be maintained by concealing the face, seems to have been borrowed from the House-builder Moth, which is a perfect model of female excellence, according to Oriental notions, always staying at home, always hiding her face, and always producing enormous families. Perhaps the male may be attracted to the female by some peculiar instinct, for the eyes can have little to do with the discovery, she being so closely shut up in her house, and never leaving, it till the day of her death.

Tufted Spider and Sperical Spider's Nest

The Tufted Spider of the West Indies spins a large, oval, cocoon-like nest. This creature derives its name from the remarkable tufts of stiff, bristle-like hairs which decorate the limbs.

Of the curious Spherical Spider nests, with their black cross bars, nothing is known except the mere fact of their existence.

There is a species of spider which constructs a remarkable pensile nest, as seen in the illustration. The spider takes several concave seed-pods, and. fastens them firmly together with the silken thread of which webs are made, and in the interior the eggs are placed. In the lower part of the illustration is a leaf upon which are piled a number of fragments of leaves, so as to form a rude conical heap. This is also the work of a spider, and is made with great ingenuity, for the structure has been regularly built up of a great number of pieces, each being arranged methodically upon the other. The labor must have been considerable, even if the spider had nothing to do but to arrange and fasten together pieces of leaves which had already been selected.

The Water Spider is a most curious and interesting creature, because it affords an example of an animal which breathes atmospheric air constructing a home beneath the water, and filling it with the air needful for respiration. The sub-aquatic cell of the Water Spider may be found in many rivers and ditches, where the water does not run very swiftly. It is made of silk, as is the case with all spiders nests, and is generally egg-shaped, having an opening below. This cell is filled with air ; and if the spider be kept in a glass vessel, it may be seen reposing in the cell, with its head downward, after the manner of its tribe. The Water Spider places her eggs in this cell, spinning a saucer-shaped cocoon, and fixing it against the inner side of the cell and near the top. In this cocoon are about a hundred eggs, of a spherical shape, and very small. The cell is a true home for the spider, which passes its earliest days under the water, and when it is strong enough to construct a sub-aquatic home for itself, brings its prey to the cell before eating it.

There is another spider which frequents the water, but which only makes a temporary and moveable residence. This is the Raft Spider, which is represented in the illustration of its natural size. Not content with chasing insects on land, it follows them in the water, on the surface of which it can run freely. It needs, however, a resting-place, and forms one by getting together a quantity of dry leaves and similar substances, which it gathers into a rough ball, and fastens with silken threads. On this ball the spider sits, and allows itself to be blown about the water by the wind. Apparently it has no means of directing its course but suffers its raft to traverse the surface as the

Pensile Spider's Nest

wind or current may carry it. The spider does not merely sit upon the raft, and there capture any prey that may happen to come within reach, but when it sees an insect upon the surface, it leaves the raft, runs swiftly over the water, secures its prey, and brings it back to the raft. It can even descend below the surface of the water, and will often crawl several inches in depth. This feat it does not perform by diving, as is the case with the water spider, but by means of the aquatic plants, down whose stems it crawls. Its capability of existing for some time beneath the surface of the water is often the means of saving its life, for, when it sees an enemy approaching, it quietly slips under the raft, and there lies in perfect security until the danger has passed away.

The Raft Spider

As a rule, fishes display but little architectural genius, their anatomical construction debarring them from raising any but the simplest edifice. A fish has but one tool, its mouth, and even this instrument is of very limited capacity. Still, although the nest which a fish can make is necessarily of a slight and rude character, there are some members of that class which construct houses which deserve the name. The best examples of architecture among fishes are those which are produced by the Stickle-backs, those well-known little beings whose spiny bodies, brilliant colors, and dashing courage make them such favorites with all who study nature. These fishes make their nests of the delicate vegetation that is found in fresh water, and will carry materials from some little distance in order to complete the home. The materials of which the nest is made are extremely variable, but they are always constructed so as to harmonize with the surrounding objects, and thus to escape ordinary observation. Sometimes it is made of bits of grass which have been blown into the river, sometimes of straws, and sometimes of growing plants. The object of the nest is evident enough, when the habits of the Stickle-back are considered.

Fifteen Spined Stickleback and Nest

As is the case with many other fish, there are no more determined destroyers of Stickle-back eggs than the Stickle-backs themselves, and the nests are evidently constructed for the purpose of affording a resting place for the eggs until they are hatched. If a few of these nests be removed from the water in a net, and the eggs thrown into the stream, the Stickle-backs rush at them from all sides, and fight for them like boys scrambling for half-pence. The eggs are very small, barely the size of dust-shot, and are yellow when first placed in the nest, but deepen in color as they approach maturity.

Corals and Madrepores

There is a well-known marine species of this group, called the Fifteen-Spined Stickle-back, a long-bodied, long snouted fish, with a slightly projecting lower jaw, and a row of fifteen short and sharp spines along the back. This creature makes its nest of the smaller algae, and the delicate green and purple sea-weeds which fringe our coasts. Sometimes, indeed, it becomes rather eccentric in its architecture, and builds in very curious situations. A case is on record where a pair of Stickle -backs had made their nest in the loose end of a rope, from which the separated strands hung out about a yard from the surface, over a depth of four or five fathoms, and to which the materials could only have been brought, of course, in the mouth of the fish, from the distance of about thirty feet. They were formed of the usual aggregation of the finer sorts of green and red sea-weed, but they were so matted together in the hollow formed by the untwisted strands of the rope that the mass constituted an oblong ball of nearly the size of the fist, in which had been deposited the scattered assemblage of spawn, and which was bound into shape with a thread of animal substance, which was passed through and through in various directions, while the rope itself formed an outside covering to the whole.

The wonderful creatures which are classed together under the general term of Corals, are familiar to us either in a manufactured state or as ornaments for the drawing-room. How vast are their submarine labors is evident from the enormous "coral-reefs" which they raise, and which for great islands whereon an army can live, and inlets wherein a fleet can ride securely at anchor. The young Coral animal passes through various changes, gradually developing new and remarkable powers, until it arrives at its perfection. The precise connection which exists between the animal and its coral habitation may not be generally understood. If the reader will take up a branch of the ordinary coral of commerce, he will see that it is slightly grooved or fluted throughout its extent, and that its surface is studded with little projections having star-like discs. Now, if this piece of coral could be again clothed with the living creature by which it was deposited, we should see a beautiful and a wonderful sight. Next to the stony corel lie a series of longitudinal vessels, each vessel corresponding with a groove, and above them lies a confused mass of irregular vessels communicating with each other. At intervals there arise the lovely flowerets of the Coral, the bodies being bright rose-color, and their arms pure white. These arms or tentacles are in ceaseless motion, and the aspect of a large and healthy branch of coral is imposingly beautiful. The animal has the power of depositing certain minute calcareous particles, commonly called spicules, which are always of remarkable forms, and are different in the various species of coral. In the common red coral they are nearly cylindrical, and armed with projecting knobs covered with angular spikes. These spicules are then bound together by a red cement, and thus the coral is formed, the fluted branches being deposited under the longitudinal vessels, and the raised projections under the flowerets of the polyp. To see the coral in full vigor it is necessary to visit the spots where it grows, as it dies almost immediately after being taken out of the water, and even if transferred with great care to a vessel is sure to die in a very short time. Several of the more curious species of Corals and Madrepores are to be seen in illustration, which represents a portion of sea-bed beset with these beautiful zoophytes. To a few of these only we can allude in this article. Toward the centre of the illustration, and on the right-hand side, may be seen a remarkable tree-like object, covered with long, tendril-like appendages, each tipped with a radiating beard. This zoophyte is known by the title of *Xenia elongata,* and on account of its singular form is a very conspicuous species. Examples of this genus are spread over many of the hotter parts of the world, some being found in the Red Sea, and all notable for the remarkable form of the animal and its submarine home. The present species has been chosen more for the singularity of its form than the beauty of its colors, which can not be expressed in the simple black and white of a wood-cut. Some species of this genus have the star-like tentacles colored with blue of various shades, some with rose, and some with lilac; and as in many cases the expanded tentacles are an inch in diameter, the effect of a large mass of these animals in full health is very fine. In the left-hand lower corner of the illustration is a curious globular object, covered with circular and radiated marks, and having a number of flower-headed projections upon the top. This is the *Green Astroea,* one of the finest examples of a singular and beautiful group of zoophytes. The color of this species is simple and pleasing. The body of the animal is pale gray-blue, and the tentacles are bright green, so that when a number of the animals are simultaneously protruding themselves the general effect is very striking. These zoophytes are able to retract themselves almost wholly within their houses, so that nothing is visible except that round the mouth there is a small green circle, which is formed by the projecting tips of the tentacles. In the left centre of the illustration is seen a group of that most beautiful zoophyte which is known as the Red Organ-pipe Coral. This handsome zoophyte is found chiefly off Carteret, in New Ireland, and is grouped together in masses that are often many yards in diameter. It is usually found in about two or three feet of water, but is some-times placed so high that at very low tides it is laid bare by the receding waters. The animal which forms this wonderful tubing is cylindrical, and the tentacles are pinkish, not possessing the brilliant red of the tubes, and in its native state the animals envelop so completely the upper part of the general mass that the bright red head is not perceptible. The coral masses are very fragile, and will not bear the pressure of the human foot, crumbling beneath the tread as if they were made of sugar. The tubes are beautifully cylindrical, and do not adhere to each other, being kept asunder by partitions, which precisely resemble the boards through which the pipes of an organ are passed.

Passing from these minute creatures, we can not forbear giving one or two additional illustrations of curious homes among the Mammalia. The Beavers afford an excellent example of animals, not only social by dwelling near each other, but by joining in a work which is for the benefit of the community. Water is as needful for the Beaver as for the miller, and it is a very curious fact that long before millers ever invented dams, or before men ever learned to grind corn, the Beaver knew how to make a dam and insure itself a constant supply of water. That the Beaver does make a dam is a fact that has long been familiar, but how it sets to work is not so well known. Engravings representing the Beavers and their habitations are common enough, but they are generally untrustworthy, not having been drawn from the natural object but from the imagination of the artist. In order to comprehend the mode of its structure we must watch the Beaver at work. When the animal has fixed upon a tree which it believes to be suitable for its purpose it begins by sitting upright, and with its chisel-like teeth cutting a bold groove completely round the trunk. It then widens the groove, and always makes it wide in exact proportion to its depth, so that when the tree is nearly cut through it looks something like the contracted portion of an hour-glass. When this stage has been reached the Beaver looks anxiously at the tree, and views it on every side, as if desirous of measuring the direction in which it is to fall. Having settled this question it goes to the opposite side of the tree, and with two or three powerful bites cuts away the wood, so that the tree becomes overbalanced and falls to the ground. This point having been reached, the animal proceeds to cut up the fallen trunk into lengths, usually a yard or so in length, employing a similar method of severing the wood. In consequence of this mode of gnawing the timber both ends of the logs are rounded and rather pointed, as may be seen by reference to the illustration. The dam is by no means placed at random in the stream, just where a few logs may have happened to lodge, but is set exactly where it is wanted, and is made so as to suit the force of the current. In those places where the stream runs slowly the dam is carried straight across the river, but in those where the water has much power the barrier is made in a convex shape, so as to resist the force of the rushing water. The power of the stream can, therefore, always be inferred from the shape of the dam which the Beavers have built across it. Some of these structures are of very great size, measuring two or three hundred yards in length, and ten or twelve feet in thickness, and their form exactly corresponds with the force of the stream. The Beaver makes its houses close to the water, and communicates with it by means of subterranean passages, one entrance of which passes into the house or "lodge," as it is technically named, and the other into the water, so far below the surface that it can not be dosed by ice. It is, therefore, always possible for the Beaver to gain access to the provision stores, and to return to its house, without being seen from the land.

The Beaver and Its Home

The lodges are nearly circular in form, and much resemble the well known snow-houses of the Esquimaux, being domed, and about half as high as they are wide, the average height being three

75

feet and the diameter six or seven feet. These are the interior dimensions, the exterior measurement being much greater, on account of the great thickness of the walls, which are continually strengthened with mud and brandies, so that during the severe frosts they are nearly as hard as solid stone. Each lodge will accommodate several individuals, whose beds are arranged around the walls. Generally, the Beavers desert their huts in the summer time, although one or two of the houses may be occupied by a mother and her young offspring. All the old Beavers who have no domestic ties to chain them at home take to the water, and swim up and down the stream at liberty, until the month of August, when they return to their homes.

The Elk, or Moose, inhabits the northern parts of America and Europe, and is, consequently, an animal which is formed to endure severe cold. Although a very large and powerful animal, measuring sometimes seven feet in height at the shoulders—a height which is very little less than that of an average elephant—it has many foes, and is much persecuted both by man and beast. In summer time it is tolerably safe, but in the winter it is beset by many perils. During the sharp frosts, also, the Elk runs but little risk, because it can traverse the hard, frozen surface of the snow with considerable speed, although with a strange, awkward gait. But when the milder weather begins to set in it is in constant danger. The warm sun falling on the snow produces a rather curious effect. The frozen surface only partially melts, and, the water, mixing with the snow beneath, causes it to sink away from the icy surface, leaving a considerable space between them. The "crust," as the frozen surface is technically named, is quite strong enough to bear the weight of comparatively small animals, such as wolves, especially when they run swiftly over it; but it yields to the enormous weight of the Elk, which plunges to its belly at every step. The wolves have now the Elk at an advantage. They can overtake it without the least difficulty; and if they can bring it to bay in the snow its fate is sealed. They care little for the branching horns, but leap boldly at the throat of the hampered

The Elk

animal, whose terrible fore-feet are now powerless, and, by dint of numbers, soon worry it to death. Man, too, takes advantage of this state of the snow, equips himself with snow-shoes, and skims over the slight and brittle crust with perfect security. An Elk, therefore, whenever abroad in the snow, is liable to many dangers, and, in order to avoid them, it makes the curious temporary habitation called the Elk yard, and which is represented in the illustration. This winter home is very simple in construction, consisting of a large space of ground on which the snow is trampled down by continually treading it so as to form both a hard surface on which the animal can walk, and a kind of fortress in which it can dwell securely. The whole of the space is not trodden down to one uniform level, but consists of a network of roads or passages through which the animal can pass at ease. So confident is the Elk in the security of the "yard" that It can scarcely ever be induced to leave its snowy fortification and pass into the open ground. This habit renders it quite secure from the attacks of wolves, which prowl about the outside of the yard, but dare not venture within; but, unfortunately for the Elk, the very means which preserve it from one danger only lead it into another. If the hunter can come upon one of these Elk-yard's he is sure of his quarry; for the animal will seldom leave the precincts of the snowy inclosure, and the rifle-ball soon lays low the helpless.

The Elk is not the only animal that makes these curious fortifications, for a herd of Wapiti deer will frequently unite in forming a common home. One of these "yards" has been known to measure between four and five miles in diameter, and to be a perfect network of paths sunk in the snow. So deep, indeed, is the snow when untrodden, that when the deer traverse the paths, their backs can not be seen above the level of the white surface which conceals the yard.

Burrowing Animals

Fortress of the Mole

THE wonderful ingenuity evinced by many animals in the construction of their homes has led the naturalist to persevering researches in tracing out the haunts and ways of those not familiarly known.

It is not often that the lover of nature has opened to him such a rare and curious museum as is exhibited in the volume from which the materials of this article are drawn. The author tells of strange habitations, made without hands, beneath, above, and around us— burrows, nests, and curious domiciles of every kind, in earth, air, and water. Nor are these presented to the mental vision merely, but are so clearly and elegantly illustrated, that we almost fancy that these strange dwelling-places are really before the eye.

It is impossible, within the limits of a single article, to do more than present to the reader a few specimens of these homes—and these are selected from the Burrowers—whose secret localities are rarely known.

Yet the burrow is the simplest form of habitation, whether it is in the ground, or in stone, wood, or any other substance.

Among mammalia, the Mole ranks first in the list of burrowers. This extraordinary animal, which is found both in Europe and America, forms a complicated subterranean dwelling-place, with chambers, passages, and other arrangements of wonderful completeness. It has regular roads leading to its feeding-grounds; establishes a system of communication as elaborate as that of a modern railway, or, to be more correct, as that of the subterranean network of metropolitan sewers ; and is an animal of varied accomplishments.

It can run tolerably fast, fight like a bull-dog, capture prey under or above ground, swim fearlessly, and can sink wells for the purpose of quenching its thirst. Take the mole out of its proper sphere, and it is awkward and clumsy; but replace it in the familiar earth, and it becomes a different being—full of life and energy, and actuated by a fiery activity which seems quite inconsistent with its dull aspect and seemingly inert form.

The absence of any external indication of eyes communicates a peculiar dullness to the creature's look, and the formation of the fore limbs gives an indescribable awkwardness to its gait.

We need not pity the mole for the dull life we suppose it leads below the ground. There it is happy, and there only can it develop its various capabilities. No one can witness the eagerness with which it flings itself upon its prey, and the evident enjoyment with which it consumes its hapless victim, without perceiving that the creature is exultantly happy in its own peculiar way.

The ordinary mole-hills present nothing particularly worthy of notice. They are the shafts through which the quadrupedal miner ejects the materials which it has scooped out, as it drives its many tunnels through the soil, and if they be carefully opened after the rain has consolidated the heap of loose material, nothing more will be discovered than a simple hole leading into the tunnel. But if we strike into one of the large tunnels, and follow it up, we come to the real abode of the, animal. A section of this extraordinary habitation, hidden under a hillock of considerable size, is given in the illustration on the preceding page.

The central apartment is a nearly spherical chamber, the roof of which is nearly on a level with the earth around the hill, and therefore situated at a considerable depth from the apex of the heap. Around this are driven two circular galleries—one just level with the ceiling, and the other at some height above. The upper circle is much smaller than the lower. Five short descending passages connect the galleries with each other, but the only entrance into the inner apartment is from the upper gallery, out of which three passages lead into the ceiling. It will be seen, therefore, that when a mole enters the house from one of his tunnels, he has first to get into the lower gallery, to ascend thence to the upper gallery, and so descend into his chamber.

There is, however, another entrance from below, by a passage which dips downward from the centre of the chamber, and then, faking a curve upward, opens into one of the larger tunnels.

The use of so complicated a series of cells and passages is extremely doubtful, since there is reason to believe that the owner, instead of retiring to his fortress to rest, often contents himself with lying in the high-road. Wonderful as is this subterraneous abode, it is not the only one constructed by this animal. A nursery is provided, more extended, though simpler, inlaid with dried grass, and intersected by many passages, so that the mother and young may easily escape from any apprehended danger. The walls of all these passages are rendered smooth and hard by the pressure of the mole's fur, so that the earth will not fall in after the severest storm.

The whole life of the mole is one of fury, and he eats like a starving tiger, tearing and rending his prey with claws and teeth, and crunching audibly the body of the worms between the sharp points. A mole has been seen to fling itself upon a small bird, tear its body open, and devour it while still palpitating with life. Nothing short of this fiery energy could sustain an animal in the lifelong task of forcing itself through the solid earth.

A battle between two moles is as tremendous as one between two lions, if not more so, because the mole is more courageous than the lion, and, relatively speaking, is far more powerful and armed with weapons more destructive. Magnify the mole to the size of the lion, and you will have a beast more terrible than the world has yet seen. Though nearly blind, it would be active beyond conception, leaping with lightning quickness upon any animal which it met, and rending it to pieces in a moment. Such a creature would, without the least hesitation, devour a serpent twenty feet in length, and so terrible would be its voracity that it would eat twenty or thirty of such snakes in the course of a day.

When fighting with one of his own species the mole gives his whole energies to the destruction of his opponent, without seeming to heed the injuries which are inflicted upon himself, exhibiting an extraordinary amount of muscular power concentrated into a very small space.

The mole emerges from the earth with unsoiled fur. This cleanliness is due in part to the peculiar character of the hair, and partly to strong membraneous muscle beneath the skin, by means of which the animal gives itself a frequent and powerful shake.

There are many burrowing animals, but the mole is emphatically the burrower—the very type of a creature which is intended to pass the whole of an active existence under ground. He absolutely riots in the exuberance of animal spirits and muscular activity, passing through the earth almost like a fish through the water, and giving to its strange and apparently sombre life a poetry and an interest which we fail to find in the lives of many creatures more richly endowed with external beauty.

The Arctic Fox, an animal which dwells in the polar regions, is notable for the extent and structure of the burrow. In order to shield itself from the inclemency of the climate it digs to a considerable depth; and it is rather remarkable that a solitary burrow is seldom found, twenty or thirty foxes generally sinking their tunnels in close proximity to each other.

"Earth" of the Fox

If one of these little colonies could be laid open a very curious sight would present itself. The earth would be seen to be pierced with multitudinous tunnels, each complete and independent in itself, and never interfering with burrows belonging to other owners. Each burrow, too, is of a very complex character, consisting of three or four distinct passages, each of which opens into a common chamber of considerable dimensions. There is also a separate nursery, communicating by a passage with this chamber, where four or five young are reared.

Nests of Birds, Insects and Animals

The Arctic Fox has been subjected to a merciless persecution on account of the value of its skin ; and consequently it has become so exceedingly crafty that it is caught with the greatest difficulty. Curious tales are told how they have learned to remove the baits without falling into the traps or being shot by the spring-guns.

Even in its ordinary state the skin of the Arctic Fox is in great favor as a fur; but when it is bleached by the dread cold of the regions in which the animal resides, and is of a pure snowy whiteness down to the very roots of the hair, it is so exceedingly costly that a mantle made of that fur is only to be purchased by millionaires, or placed on imperial shoulders. The fur of a fine old fox in perfect condition is worth many times its weight in gold.

The habitation of the common fox is by no means so complicated as that of the Arctic species. It avoids, when possible, the labor of burrowing, and avails itself of the deserted home of a badger, or even of a rabbit, altering and enlarging to suit its own purposes. Herein it lies asleep all day, as is the custom with most predaceous animals, and only sallies forth at night. Herein the mother produces and nurtures her young, and sometimes on a summer's evening the whole family, the father, mother, and cubs come out to enjoy the fresh air. They never wander far from the mouth of the burrow, and as the young are gamesome little creatures, as playful as puppies, and much prettier, and the mother helps her young ones in their sports as a good mother ought to do, the group presents a very pretty sight. Though there is but one burrow for the nursery the fox generally has access to "earths," as they are called, at considerable distances apart, to any one of which he will repair if danger threatens.

The Prairie Dog, so called from the short, yelping sound which it utters, is a pretty animal, about sixteen inches long. Its head is peculiarly flat, which gives it a remarkable aspect. It is an exceedingly prolific animal, multiplying rapidly, and extending its excavations to vast distances. Indeed, when one the Prairie Dogs settle themselves in a convenient spot, their increase seems to have no bounds, and the little heaps of earth which stand near the mouth of their burrows extend as far as the eye can reach. They are dug in a sloping direction, forming an angle of about forty-five degrees with the horizon, and after descending for five or six feet, they take a sudden turn and rise gradually upward. Thousands upon thousands of these burrows are dug in close proximity to each other, and honey-comb the ground to such an extent that it is rendered quite unsafe for horses.

A Prarie Dog "Town"

The scene presented by one of these "dog towns" or "villages," as the assemblages of burrows are called, is most curious, and well repays the trouble of approaching without alarming the cautious little animals. Fortunately for the traveler the Prairie Dog is as inquisitive as it is wary, and the indulgence of its curiosity often costs the little creature its life. Perched on the hillocks, which have already, been mentioned, the Prairie Dog is able to survey a wide extent of horizon, and as soon as it sees an intruder, it gives a sharp yelp of alarm and dives into its burrow, its little feet knocking together with a ludicrous flourish as it disappears. In all directions a similar scene is enacted. Warned by the well-known cry, all the Prairie Dogs within reach repeat the call and leap into their burrows. Their curiosity, however, is irrepressible, and scarcely have their feet vanished from sight than their heads are seen cautiously protruded from the burrow, and their inquisitive brown eyes sparkle as they examine the cause of the disturbance.

The Prairie Dog has not the privilege of possessing a home for its own exclusive use; the Burrowing Owl and terrible rattlesnake take forcible possession of the burrows. Formerly it was supposed that these incongruous beings associated together in perfect harmony, forming a sort of "Happy Family" below the surface of the ground: But all these romantic notions have been dispelled by the naturalist, and the snake has been proved to be no welcome guest, but an intruder on the premises, self-billeted on the inmates like soldiers on obnoxious householders, procuring lodging without permission, and eating the inhabitants by way of board; and it is not impossible that the Owl may snap up a young and tender Prairie Dog in its early infancy.

It is well known that the rabbit lived socially in burrows—a number of them forming a warren. They seek a loose, sandy locality, where the soil is easily excavated, and where furze abounds, the young shoots of which furnish them with nutritious food. When once established they increase with incredible rapidity. The creature becomes a parent at a very early age; and by the time a rabbit is a year old, it may have attained the dignity of a grand-parent. She does not produce her young in any of the burrows to which the general rabbit colony has access, but prepares an isolated tunnel, at the end of which she forms her nest. The bed on which the young recline is beautifully soft and fine, being composed chiefly of the downy fur which grows on the mother's breast, and which she plucks off with her teeth in tufts of considerable size.

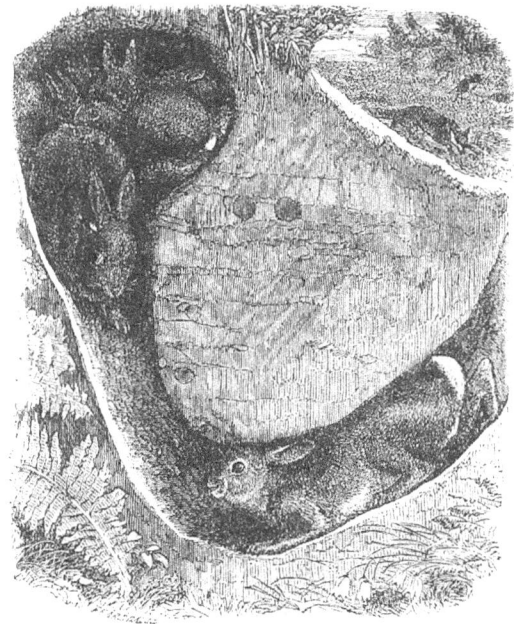

The Rabbit Warren

The Polar Bear makes its curious burrow in a peculiar substance, and is worthy of special notice. Toward the month of December, she retreats to the side of a rock, where, by dint of scraping, and allowing the snow to fall upon her, she forms a cell in which to reside during the period of her *accouchement*. Within this strange nursery she produces her young, and remains with them beneath the snow until the month of March, when she emerges into the outer air,

87

bringing with her the baby bears, who are then about as large as ordinary rabbits. As the time passes on, the breath of the family, together with the warmth exhaled from their bodies, serves to enlarge the cell, so that in proportion with their increasing dimensions the accommodation is increased to suit them. As is the case with the snow-covered sheep, the hidden bear may be discovered by means of the little hole which is made by the warm breath, and is rendered more distinguishable by the hoar frost which collects around it.

The Polar Bear

This curious abode is not sought by every Polar Bear, its only use being to shelter the young. Before retiring into winter-quarters the bear eats enormously, and, driven by an unfailing instinct, resorts to the most nutritious diet, so that it becomes prodigiously fat. During the three months of her seclusion she takes no food, but exists upon the store of fat which has been accumulated before retiring to her winter home. A similar phenomenon may be, observed in many of

The Giant Armadillo

the hibernating animals, but in the bear it is more remarkable from the fact that she has not only to support her own existence, but to impart nourishment to her offspring. It is true, that in order to enable them to find sufficient food, they are of wonderfully small dimensions when compared with the parent; but the fact remains,

89

that the animal is able to lay up within itself so large a store of nutriment that it can maintain its own life and suckle its young for a space of three months without taking a morsel of food.

The various species of Armadillo are all mighty burrowers. They are carnivorous, and feed upon insects, and all kind of animal substances found below the surface of the earth. The Giant Armadillo is so determined a burrower that it has often been known to dig up dead bodies for the purpose of feeding on them. All these creatures, however, are fond of substances, and many of them may be found upon the savannas of South America, feasting greedily upon the bodies of the cattle which are slaughtered so recklessly for the sake of their hides. In all these animals the coat of mail is exceedingly hard, so hard indeed that it is used for sharpening the long Spanish knife.

The AardVark

If an Armadillo should be surprised at any time, and its retreat to its burrow intercepted, it at once commences sinking a new tunnel; and so rapidly does it excavate, that it is almost impossible to capture one. The coat of mail is perfectly flexible, giving full freedom to the limbs, and permitting the animal to roll itself into a ball when threatened with danger.

Woodpecker

The curious Aard Vark of Southern Africa resides for the most part in great holes which it scoops in the ground. The name signifies Earth-hog, and is given to the animal on account of its extraordinary powers of excavation and. the swine-like contour of its head. The claws with which this animal works are enormous, and are by no means intended merely to excavate burrows in soft or sandy soil, though they are frequently employed for that purpose. By means of these implements the Aard Vark tears to pieces the enormous ant-hills which stud the plains of Southern Africa—edifices so strongly

91

made as to resemble stone rather than mud, and capable of bearing the weight of many men on their summits. These marvelous dwellings are absolutely swarming with inmates; and it is for the purpose of feeding upon the tiny builders that the Aard Vark plies its destructive labors.

Kingfisher's Nest

Toward evening the Aard Vark issues from the burrow wherein it has lain asleep during the day, proceeds to the plains, and searches for an ant-hill in full operation. With its powerful claws it tears a hole in the side of the hill, breaking up, the stony walls with perfect ease, and scattering dismay among the inmates. As the ants run hither and thither, in consternation, their dwelling falling like a city shaken by an earthquake, the author of all this misery flings its slimy tongue among them, and sweeps them into its mouth by hundreds.

Among the feathered burrowers the Sand-Martin, so common in

England, is an excellent example. Few would suppose that the tiny bill of this pretty little bird was capable of boring tunnels into sandstone. The Sand-Martin, however, prefers an easy task, when that is possible, and will always avail itself of a locality where the soil is loose, and yet where the sides of the burrow will not collapse. Having fixed upon a suitable spot, it commences to work in a circular direction, using its legs as a pivot, and by dint of turning round and round, and pecking away as it proceeds, soon chips out a tolerably circular hole. After the bird has lived for some time in the tunnel the shape of the entrance is much damaged by incessant passing to and fro of the inmates; but while the burrow is still new and untenanted its form is almost cylindrical. In all cases the tunnel slopes gently upward, so as to prevent the lodgment of rain.

At the furthest extremity of the burrow, which is always rather larger than the shaft, is placed the nest, a very simple structure, upon which are laid the eggs, which are very small, and of a delicate pinky whiteness.

Few foes can injure the Sand-Martin during incubation, because of the difficulty of gaining admission to the nest.

Man is perhaps its worst enemy, for there is a mixture of adventure and danger in taking the eggs, which is irresistible to the British school-boy. To climb up a perpendicular rock, to cling with one hand, while the other is thrust into the burrow, and to know that a chance slip will certainly snap the invading arm like a tobacco-pipe stem, is a combination of joys which no well-conditioned boy can withstand.

The illustration shows the nest of the Kingfisher, which, although it does not excavate the whole of the burrow in which it resides, alters and arranges a ready-made burrow to suit its own necessities.

The Storing Petrel, that bird of ill omen, as the sailors think it, digs its little burrow in the sandy soil, and there conceals itself and its treasure—a single egg.

Formerly the Woodpecker was reckoned among the enemies of

the forest. But now it is generally known that the common species is unable to cut through sound wood, but chooses a decayed tree, in which its pick-axe like beak is able easily to make its burrow. The burrowing powers of the Ivory-billed Woodpecker are marvelous, its chisel-like beak having been known to chip splinters from a mahogany table, and to cut a hole fifteen inches in width through a lath-and-plaster partition.

Toucan

The Toucan is remarkable for its enormous bill, which is decorated with brilliant tints of orange and black, scarlet and yellow, or red and green—varying in different species. Whether this huge beak is the tool with which it excavates its burrow is uncertain. It is said, however, that the young of the Toucan, being liable to the attacks of monkeys and birds of prey, whenever the parent bird is alarmed, all she has to do is to poke her beak out of the aperture leading to her nest. The assailant, seeing so huge a bill, fancies an animal of corresponding size behind it, and hastily flees.

Petrel

Among the crustacea the Land Crab is fully entitled to be ranked in the class of burrowers. Its singular habits are, however, more familiarly known than those of the Robber Crab a creature of strange, weird shape, difficult to describe, but easily comprehended by reference to the illustration. The Robber Crab inhabits the Indian Ocean. It does not live in a shell, but its abdomen is protected by hard plates. It is a quick walker, although rather awkward in its gait, impeded probably by the enormous claws. While walking it presents a curious aspect, being lifted nearly a foot above the ground on its two central pairs of legs; and if it be intercepted in its retreat it brandishes its formidable weapons, clattering them loudly, and always keeping its face toward the enemy.

The food of the Robber Crab is of a very peculiar nature, consisting mostly, if not entirely, of the cocoa-nut. It seizes upon the

The Robber Crab

fallen cocoa-nuts, and with its enormous pincers tears away the outer covering, reducing it to a mass of raveled threads. This substance is carried by the crabs into their holes, for the purpose of forming a bed. When the crab has freed the nut from the husk it introduces the small end of a claw into one of the little holes which are found at one end of the cocoa-nut, and by turning the claw backward and forward, as if it were a brad-awl, the crab contrives to scoop out the soft substance of the nut. These crabs burrow in the earth under the roots of the trees that furnish them with provisions, prudently storing up in their holes large quantities of cocoa-nuts, stripped of their husk, at those times when the fruits are most abundant, against the recurring intervals when they are scarce.

Prolas in Wood and Rock

It is stated that if the long and delicate antennae of these robust creatures be touched with oil, they instantly die. They are not found on any of these islands except the small coral ones, of which they are the principal occupants.

This crab is more than two feet in length when full grown, and is accounted delicious food.

The Pholas, one of the marine burrowing molluscs, has an

extremely fragile shell, of rather soft texture, and its outer surface is covered with ridges, which sweep in graceful curves from the hinge to the edge, and bear some resemblance to the projections upon a file. By means of these tiny points the Pholas is able to work its way into rock, using his shell as a sort of brad-awl. Some species bore into wood, but always across the grain; while the Shipworm, whose ravages often produce such disastrous consequences, always bores with the grain of the wood. When the Shipworm first issues from the sheltering mantle of its parent it is a little, round, lively object, covered with cilia, like a very minute hedgehog, but it speedily changes into a worm-like mollusc nearly a foot in length. It devours wood of every description, often taking possession of a piece of timber and wholly destroying it; thus being the hidden cause of numerous wrecks.

Shipworm

Of all the burrowing spiders none is so admirable an excavator as the Trap-door Spider of Jamaica, and none displays so much ingenuity in the arrangement of its burrow. When the earth which surrounds it is removed, a double silken tube is found, the outer portion being thick, harsh, and crumpled, looking more like the rough bark of a tree than a spider's web. The inner layer is of a very different character. This is uniformly smooth to the eye, and of a silken softness to the touch. The texture of the interior surface is quite unlike that of the inner or outer tube, being nearly white and of a smoothness and consistency much resembling rough and unsized paper. It is curiously stiff also, and is so formed that no one who saw it for the first time would be likely to guess at its real character. The entrance of the tube is guarded by the "trap-door," from which the spider takes its name. This is a flap of the same substance as the tube, circular in shape, so as to fit the orifice with perfect accuracy, and attached to the tube by a tolerably wide hinge, so that when it closes it does not fall to either side, but comes true and fair upon the opening which it defends. The inner surface of the trap-door is white and felt-like, and exactly resembles the interior of the tube, but its outer surface is covered with earth, taken from the soil in which the hole is dug. As the trap-door is flush with the surface of the ground, it is evident that, when it is closed, all traces of the burrow, and its inhabitant are lost.

The spider is urged by a curious instinct to make its tunnel in some sloping spot, and to keep the hinge uppermost, so that when the inhabitant leaves its home, or retreats to the extremity of its burrow, the door closes of its own accord, and effectually conceals it. Newcomers into the country which the Trap-door Spider inhabits are often surprised by seeing the ground open, a little lid lifted up, and a rather formidable spider peer about, as if to reconnoiter the position before leaving its fortress. At the least movement on the part of the spectator back pops the spider, like the cuckoo on a clock, clapping its little door after it quite as smartly as the wooden bird, and in most cases succeeds in evading the search of the astonished observer, the soil being apparently unbroken, without a trace of the curious little door that had been so quickly shut.

Even if the little door should be found, it requires some force to open it, for the ingenious creature secures it on the inside, probably by holding it down with his claws, which are very powerful.

The Trap Door Spider and Nests

Nothing short of actual violence will induce the Trap-door Spider to vacate the premises which it so courageously defends. It will permit the earth to be excavated around its burrow, and the whole nest to be removed, without deserting its home; and in this manner

100

specimens have been removed and placed in positions where their proceedings could be watched.

Without going into the details of its construction, we give an illustration showing the nest of the common, Humble Bee (familiarly called Bumble Bee), which is usually in the side of some bank of earth; and of the Lapidary Bee, which makes its nest either in the ground or within a heap of stones.

Bumble Bee   Lapidary Bee

There is one well known and handsome insect which is greatly disliked by almost every one. Yet the habitation of this insect is a marvel of ingenious industry. Let us fancy ourselves watching the construction of its nest. In the early days of spring, a Wasp issues from the place in which it has passed the winter, and anxiously surveys the country. She does not fly fast nor high, but passes slowly and carefully along, examining every earth bank, and entering every crevice to which she comes.

At last she finds a burrow made by a field mouse, or perhaps strikes upon the deserted tunnel of some large burrowing insect, enters it, stays a long while within, comes out again and fusses about outside, enters again, and seems to make up her mind. In fact, she is house-hunting, and all her movements are very like those of a careful matron selecting a new home.

Having thus settled upon a convenient spot, she proceeds to form a chamber, at some depth from the surface, breaking away the soil, and carrying it out piece by piece. When she has thus fashioned the chamber to her mind—for she has a mind—she flies off again, and makes her way to an old wooden fence which has stood for many years, and which, although not rotten, is perfectly seasoned. On this she settles, and, after running up and down for a little time, she fixes upon some spot, and begins to gnaw away the fibres, working with all her might, so eagerly engaged that even were we not invisible we might stand by and watch her proceedings. At last she has gathered a little bundle of fibres, which she gnaws and works about until she reduces them to a kind of pulp, and then flies back to the burrow.

She now runs up the side of the chamber, and clings to its roof with the two last pairs of legs, while with the first pair, aided by her jaws, she fixes the woody pulp on the roof, kneading it until it forms a kind of little pillar. Another and another supply is brought, until this pillar, which is pendent from the roof, like a *papier-maché* stalactite, is completed. The wasp now begins to form the comb, and at the end of the pillar she places three very shallow cells, of a cup-like shape, not hexagonal, as are the completed cells. In each of these little cups she deposits an egg, and then constructs a roof over them, made from the same material as the cells, but laid in a different manner, the length of the fibres being nearly at right angles to the centre of the proposed comb. More cells are then added, eggs are laid in them, and the roof extended over them. The eggs first laid are soon hatched, producing tiny grubs; the parent wasp meanwhile proceeds in her task of building the nest, depositing eggs, and feeding these ever-hungry grubs. In due time the oldest of them cease to feed, spin a silken cover over their cells, and after a short retirement come forth as wasps to aid their mother in some of her labors.

When the first cell terrace is full the wasps construct several pendent pillars, and form a second terrace below the first. A third fourth, and fifth are added as required, the cells being very small. The wasps that come from these cells are small, and are the workers. Larger cells are then prepared for the purpose of hatching the grubs which will become perfect male and female wasps. These come out near the end of the season.

A large nest will contain seven or eight thousand cells, and on the average each cell is the birth-place of three generations. It seems wonderfully that so slight a habitation will endure such a weight. At the end of the season the wasps abandon their nest, and most of them die. The few who remain creep into some crevice, and lie dormant until the following spring, when they emerge to be the queens and mothers of future colonies.

The strength and perseverance of the Beetle is well known. The Sexton, or Burping Beetles, accomplish their work mostly at night. Having found some dead bird, for example, they burrow entirely beneath it, scrape out the loose soil, walk round the bird, mount it as if to see how the work is proceeding, and then disappear afresh and renew their labors. Sometimes they dig rather too much on one side, and then they appear sadly puzzled, running round and round the bird, getting on it as if to press it down with their weight, pulling it this way and that way; but they resume their work until the hole is large enough to allow the bird to sink into it.

The time occupied in the transaction necessarily varies, according to the size of the buried object and the condition of the beetle; but on the average an ordinary finch, or a mouse, can be buried in the course of a day. When the task is completed a number of eggs are laid upon the buried animal, and then the beetles emerge, cover it with earth, and then fly away.

Burying Beetle   Scarabaeus   Ant Nest

The Egyptian Scarabæus sinks, a deep perpendicular hole in the ground, and having deposited an egg in a portion of soil, which she forms into a rude ball, begins a curious and laborious task. Seizing the ball between her hind-feet, she begins to roll it about in the hot sunshine, not taking it direct to the shaft which she has sunk, but remaining near the spot. Should rain come on she ceases to roll; or should the ball be made just before sunset she waits for the morning before recommencing her labor. The consequence of all this curious rolling about is twofold ; it accelerates the hatching of the inclosed egg by the exposure to the sunbeams, and it forms a thin, hard, clay-like crust round the soft material in which the egg reposes.

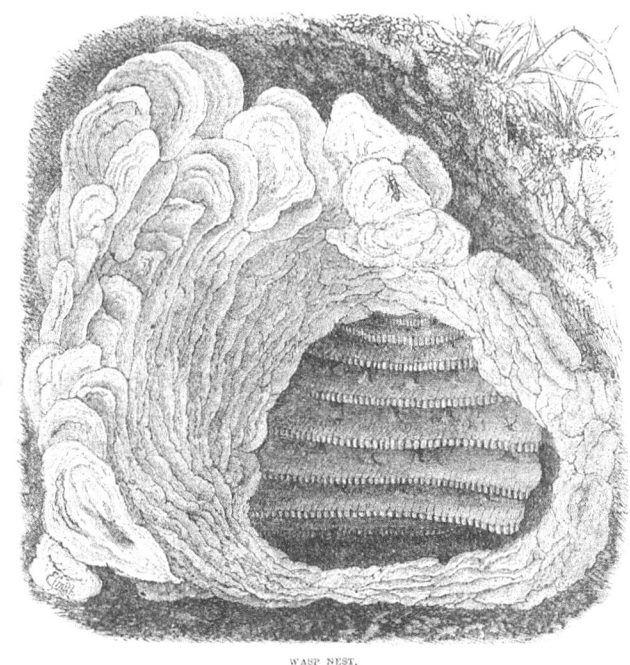

WASP NEST.

When the ball is sufficiently rolled it is taken to the hole; dropped down, and the earth filled in. The egg is very soon hatched, and from it proceeds a little white grub, which finds itself at once in the midst of food, and begins to eat vigorously. By the time it has devoured the whole of the contents of its cocoon—if the mere empty shell may be so called—it is ready for its change into the pupal form, and there lies in the earth until it again changes its form and becomes a perfect beetle.

If the reader will refer to the plate, he will there see two of these beetles at work upon a ball, for it is not an unusual circumstance that two insects should propel the same ball.

Also in the closing illustration may be seen the completed cocoon of this beetle, as well as an extraordinary cocoon of an insect called the Goliath. This specimen is in the British Museum, and is as large as a swan's egg. It is strengthened by a remarkable belt, which runs around its centre. A common house-fly is introduced into the drawing, in order to show the comparative size of the cocoon and the insect.

In the illustration we have three excellent examples of wood-boring insects. Passing by the Spirifer and Saperda which, are curious looking creatures we will describe only the dwelling constructed by the splendid South African Carpenter Bee, a wood-borer of great power. In the centre of the drawing is seen a portion of a tunnel which is completely hollowed out, and divided into cells. This is the nest of the Carpenter Bee.

Carpenter Bee. Spirifer. Saperda

When the insect has fixed upon a piece of wood which suits her purpose, usually the trunk or branch of a dead tree, an old post, or a piece of wooden railing, she bores a circular hole about an inch and a

106

half in length, and large enough to permit her to pass. Suddenly she turns at an angle, and drives her tunnel parallel to the grain of the Wood, and makes a burrow of several inches in length. None of the chips and fragments are wasted, but are carried aside and carefully stored up in some secure place, sheltered from the action of the wind.

The tunnel having now been completed, the industrious insect seeks rest in change of employment, and sets off in search of honey and pollen. With these materials she makes a little heap at the bottom of the tunnel, and deposits an egg upon the food which she has so carefully stored.

Then she proceeds to construct above the inclosed egg a ceiling, which shall be the floor of another cell. For this purpose she goes off to her store of chips, and fixes them in a ring above the heap of pollen, cementing them together with a glutinous substance, which is probably secreted by herself. A second ring is then placed inside the first, and in this manner the insect proceeds until she has made a nearly flat ceiling of concentric rings. The thickness of each ceiling is about equal to that of a penny.

The number of cells is extremely variable, but on the average each tunnel contains seven or eight, and the insect certainly makes more than one tunnel. As each tunnel generally exceeds a foot in length, and the diameter is large enough to admit the passage of the wide-bodied insect who makes it, the amount of labor performed by the bee is truly wonderful. The jaws are the only boring instruments used, and though they are strong and sharp, they scarcely seem to be adequate to the work for which they are destined.

In the illustration the upper part of one of these tunnels is shown, and in the two uppermost tells the egg has not been hatched. In the lower cells the young larva is given in order to show the attitude in which it passes its early life. When all is complete the entrance is closed.

We have given examples of several classes of habitations, while there are many other kinds equally curious; which can not fail of affording rich entertainment to those who have any taste for the Marvels of Nature. From this abundant store-house we propose hereafter to present other dwellings built by other handless architects.

Cocoons of Scarabaeus and Goliath